a pale but...
Splendid Morning

a pale but...
Splendid Morning

Jean Marie Langevin

Dear Irene —
May God's Mother fill your heart with peace and joy.
Sister Jean Marie, OSB

Our Sunday Visitor, Inc.
Huntington, Indiana 46750

©Copyright by Our Sunday Visitor, Inc. 1974
All rights reserved. No part of this book may be reproduced or transmitted in any form or by any means, electronic or mechanical, including photocopying, recording or by any information storage and retrieval system, without permission in writing from the Publisher.

ISBN: 0-87973-779-4
Library of Congress Catalog Card Number: 73-89574

Cover Design by Larry W. Lewis
Painting by James E. McIlrath

Published, printed and bound in the U.S.A. by
Our Sunday Visitor, Inc.
Noll Plaza
Huntington, Indiana   46750

*Dedicated
with love
to my brothers
Paul, Joe, Rod and Ed*

PREFACE

Spiritual books, like characters, have their individuality. They are written by scores of people who want to communicate. The reflections in this book have been composed for the casual reader. There are no startling messages in its pages — nothing that has not been said in the past.

It was written to give courage and comfort to those in the world who need to be reassured that God is still with them in the everyday happenings — that He loves them and will always do so. The spirituality in many instances is unlike the "theological approach" of our day. This is an attempt to light up the dark passages of the world with faith, hope and charity. As Hans Christian Andersen has written: "Every man's life is a fairy tale, written by God's fingers."

In ordinary experiences the part God plays in the life of those He loves is like the fairy tale Andersen mentions. His strength and power are all around us, if we will only take the time in our busy lives to notice.

I would like to thank all those who helped to make this book a possible success, especially Dr. William Wehmeyer of St. Bonaventure University who took time out of his busy summer schedule to correct my writing and advise me. It was he who removed the frills that made the writing cumbersome. Also I am most grateful to Father Raymond Geiger of Erie who kept my writing from going into a spiritual tailspin by pointing out what would keep it on an even keel. Finally I wish to express my appreciation to the members of the Administration of St. Bonaventure University who permitted me to stay on their beautiful campus while working at the book.

Sister Jean Marie Langevin, O.S.B.

INTRODUCTION

At times we moderns tend to pity those people whose lives were lived in days before modern inventions. We wonder how our ancestors ever managed to go through their lives — without television, without radio, without newspapers, without motion pictures. It may seem to us that all they did was work and go through a rather dull existence. We might even consider ourselves fortunate to be living now, in this latter third of the twentieth century.

Yes, it is true — our ancestors did not have the modern electronic inventions. But what they did have was something more important than electronics — they had time to think. The farmer and his wife lived a routine life, but they had time to think about the meaning of life, and about what they should do during life. They appreciated life at its true value: as a time of test, a time of work, a time for them to "work out their salvation in fear and trembling." They had peace.

But then, into that well-ordered peaceful existence came one modern invention after another — the newspaper, the radio, television. And then the poor farmer began to read about the troubles and scandals of other people, about the contemporary crises of the world. The more he read, the more he thought — but really, the less he thought — because his mind was now full of superficial, external ideas.

In our day this process has been carried to a logical

conclusion. The mind of man, through the media of mass communications, is filled with ideas of worldly things. The mind of man is filled with such secondary thoughts that he rarely if ever thinks about the fundamentals of life. Modern living has become increasingly distracted, increasingly shallow.

For that reason it is a particular pleasure to recommend this helpful book by Sister Jean Marie, O.S.B. We are indebted to her for showing us how one can go through life with an appreciation of the ultimate meaning of what is taking place. In living and writing, by example and by pen, Sister Jean Marie demonstrates to us the ideal of the life that combines contemplation with action.

May all who read these words learn to appreciate the ultimate meaning of life — that meaning illustrated so gracefully in this book.

✠ John F. Whealon
Archbishop of Hartford

TABLE OF CONTENTS

I
SPRING

1 — Spring in Our Hearts 15
2 — Among Madonna Lilies 18
3 — If Only We Were Grateful 21
4 — Nobody Likes Me 24
5 — The Woman Who Begged 28
6 — Locked Doors 31
7 — What Would Benedict Do? 34
8 — We Should Trust Him 38
9 — Are We Indifferent to Others? 41
10 — First Things First 45
11 — Fishing Days — Dreaming Days 48
12 — Is God Dead? 53

II
SUMMER

1 — Summer Sunlight and Storms 59
2 — A Strange Gift 63
3 — Little Men in the Mountains 66
4 — Mike Swore 69
5 — God's Country 72
6 — On Changing Our Plans 76
7 — Was It Meant for Me? 80
8 — Promises to Keep 83
9 — Shadowland 88
10 — They Were an Inspiration 91
11 — When We Need Him 94

12 — Raindrops at Loretto *98*

III
AUTUMN

1 — And This Is Autumn *103*
2 — A Steeplejack *106*
3 — I Just Couldn't Say Good-bye *109*
4 — A Memory *113*
5 — Yesterday and Today *117*
6 — Faith Is a Gift *120*
7 — Friendship Is a Risk *124*
8 — An Old Typewriter *128*
9 — If We Were All Alike *131*
10 — When You Need Someone *135*
11 — He Seemed So Far Away *138*
12 — I Loved Sister Marigold *141*

IV
WINTER

1 — Winter Winds *147*
2 — Somebody Needs You *151*
3 — Silent Loveliness *155*
4 — Our Songs Are Gone *159*
5 — Life's Problems *163*
6 — Hope Lights up Dark Places *167*
7 — To Be Or Not To Be *170*
8 — Out in the Cold *174*
9 — Love Is That Way *178*
10 — Memories of Mr. Arno *182*
11 — The Nun's Story *186*
12 — The End of the Road *190*

I

Spring

*Close to my heart I fold each
lovely thing . . .
The sweet day yields; and not
disconsolate . . .
With calm impatience of the
woods, I wait . . .
For leaf and blossom, when
God gives us spring.*

— *Whittier*

1

Spring in Our Hearts

It is spring. The birds sing joyful songs while all the world of nature is emerging from the earth where it has been sleeping for months. My heart sighs, then steps back over the years to the time when I was a child.

My brothers and I found nothing more delightful than going with Pop into the woods where he tapped the maple trees in early spring. The air on sunny days was sharp and crisp, while the smell of moist earth was all about us, blending with the odor of the damp trees. Everything fascinated me. I loved every moment spent in that maple sugar grove! It was a wonderful world, a land of hope and joy. Those were the gracious days!

It is impossible to be always a child physically, or even mentally. We cannot reach any age and just remain stationary until eternity. Nor do I think we would want to. There is something ludicrous in an old-young face which is trying to shed years, striving to go back in time to the days before experience, sorrow and pain had etched lines on the face and turned bright-colored hair a softening gray. Then, too, would we always want the mind of a teen-ager, the anxiety, the eagerness to please peers, the striving and the heartbreaking loneliness, and disappointment? As for me, I would not want to go back to those turbulent days, to the endless search for something — we knew not what. I prefer the straight look into the eyes of the fascinating, unpredictable future.

But there is a spiritual springtime which we can always have until the angel of death summons us before the throne of God. We can store in the depths of our hearts the music of God's unfailing love. We can refuse to let anything lodge in our minds which will keep the fresh green of hope from being stifled. There is so much loveliness in the world that we have but to let our hearts whisper, "Open sesame!" and it is ours. Never should we cease to wonder at the beauty all about us.

However, many of us forget all this. We permit our spirituality to trail along behind us like a caboose. In our hurry we become robots of time, running through life, concentrating on the insignificant merchandise the world offers, forgetting the spiritual ornament of hope, which would keep spring in our hearts, helping us become spiritual giants. We are so busy about many things that we toss away Christ's gifts like a wealthy playboy who doesn't know the value of money. In our hurried days we trample upon God's love before it has time to grow. Why? Is it because we are afraid nearness to Christ would cramp our style, making us queer, unnatural people whom others would pity, but never love?

Because we rarely give Christ a chance, we become mediocre souls. We drift through life, never doing good, always coaxing our consciences into submission with the age-old excuse that we are no worse than our neighbor. We do not murder, steal, or commit adultery. But is this all Christ means to us? Is this the degree of holiness the Son of God wished us to attain when He hung that faraway vernal day between heaven and earth? Were there souls who watched from afar that first Good Friday, consoling themselves with the thought that they had not nailed Him to the cross? Did they perhaps think He had made their blind see, and their lame walk, but now He was firmly attached to a cross with nails, and He would never be able to help them again? Were the mercenary souls of Christ's day first cousins to the materialistic ones of today? Does our luxury-loving world think of Christ as someone who has outlived His usefulness?

The indifference of the people must have been heavy in the air that fateful day. And somehow, I think, our modern age was there too with its critical lift of eyebrows and indifferent smile.

Why has enthusiasm for the cause of the crucified Christ died in our hearts like the fragrant flowers of spring wilting in the drying field? If only we could once again feel the joy of Christ's love, the reality of His presence, we would be new men and women, always living in the springtime of His love. The Curé of Ars has aptly said: "It is always spring in the soul united to God."

2

Among Madonna Lilies

The chapel is still and peaceful during Holy Week. There is a lingering silence of sadness and loneliness, yet a deep abounding serenity. The altars are stripped of adornment, the statues are shrouded in purple. Sisters pray the Stations of the Cross and kneel absorbed in prayer, unmindful of those around them. The lamentations and lessons of Holy Week scent the air.

This is far away from the shuffling feet of noisy boys, their furtive whispers, their indifference to lessons. The contemplative part of my nature cries out for a life like the one just described, yet my assignment is to the active life.

But this is not what I wanted to write about today. Outside of our chapel is a large statue of the Pietà. It is a wonderful piece of art. And yet, the figures never set me spiritually on fire. In my mind I have made my own Pietà. Maybe it does not fulfill the expectations of an artist, but it is a Mother who lives and breathes, someone whom I feel I can reach out and touch. She has slipped into my mind as I chant the psalms of Holy Week; she has refused to leave for long periods of time.

The Evangelists have left much to the imagination in describing the burial of the Son of God. Did Mary at this time think of Bethlehem and the song of angels? She had cradled His tiny body in her arms, knowing He was her Son and her God. But this was different. As John Lynch so aptly puts it in his poem *A Woman Wrapped in Silence:*

> And this was not a night of silver stars,
> Hushed all about a cave. . . .

April winds drifted over this Mother and her dead bruised Son. They brought the scent of Madonna lilies which bloom so profusely in Palestine at this season. Everything was still as Mary looked upon the dead body of Christ.

There were deep gashes on His body and His face was twisted with pain. This blood-soaked hair and disfigured countenance, which had once been so perfect in its shining beauty, belonged to her God as well as her Son. The gaping wounds of His body cried out for the souls of the men who had inflicted them.

The words, "Mother, behold thy son: son, behold thy Mother," were very clear to her. The whole human race was leaning on her. Her Son had entrusted the world to her from the cross.

We all need the Queen of heaven and earth, especially in our day of unrest, hate and war. Perhaps God has given us the grace never to offend Him seriously. Or could it be that like Peter, we have denied Him before a world that is ever seeking happiness in wealth, power and applause? Somewhere on life's highway we have drifted away from the Son of God. We have run in the opposite direction because we fear the taunts of the crowd.

We hide from this crucified God under a strange

worldly guise. In the silence of our hearts we feel we have denied Him, perhaps even betrayed Him to the modern rabble and crowd about us. We play hide-and-seek in the forests of pleasure, trying to forget the God of Calvary. Yet, we can never run from God, for He is everywhere. It might happen that our sense of direction is so poor we can no longer find our way back to Him. To whom can we turn?

There is one who accepted sinful mankind into her arms — Mary, the Mother of God. She hears our call and will help us, just as she helped those of the early Church. With Mary as our advocate we need never fear. She takes a personal interest in each of her earthly children.

This Queen is as real today as when she walked up the hill of Calvary and stood beneath the cross, as loving as when she held the God of love, broken and bruised by men. Not only did her Son's lifeless body show her the consequence of sin, but it brought out how dearly He loved each individual soul, since He had given over His body as a ransom for them.

In our mad world of today we seek security. We invest in stocks and bonds to make enough money to spend our twilight days in comfort. Our investments for eternity should be far more important. We must put into Mary's immaculate hands our prayers, works, joys and sufferings, begging her to help us. She will never fail us. When we meet her face-to-face we will know the joy of having loved her on earth.

3

If Only We Were Grateful

The day was drab and dismal as the seventh- and eighth-grade girls stepped from the moist spring air into the warmth of the school. Holding the door was a boy from my class. But it wasn't his holding the door that caused me to wonder while I stood for a brief moment at the head of the stairs. "Five," he said, then, "Six." By the time I reached the door he had counted as far as ten. On seeing my inquiring look he proceeded to explain that he was counting the girls who would thank him for holding the door. "And out of sixty girls there were only ten who said, 'Thank you,' " was his final statement.

"There were not sixty girls," I corrected.

As we walked to church he kept up a constant chatter, but I don't remember what he said because I kept thinking of his remark, "Only ten said, 'Thank you.' "

We forget to say "thank you" to God most of our lives. I wonder if God were to count the number of Christians who thank Him for all He has done for them — would he find even that small percentage? Do we ever thank God for the gift of faith, believing that we belong to Him in a special way? We do not seem to think it is a compliment to be permitted by His Majesty the King of heaven to enter His battlefield, fighting the unseen foes, and in so doing winning a place in His kingdom for ourselves as well as others. We are not grateful. We shrug our shoulders, grin a smug little grin, and walk right past the hill of Christ's crucifixion with our eyes fixed upon the earth and the trinkets of time. As for saying "thank you" for anything, we really haven't time.

There are countless things to thank God for, yet we are so hurried that we forget. We remember to thank our friends for the smallest favors, unless we do not mind being considered thoughtless and impolite. As for God — well, He belongs to an unseen world and . . . it's a little hard to explain.

Do we ever think of Christ wending His way through the stony streets of Jerusalem, up the steep hill of Golgotha, with the screams of hate in His ears, slipping in His own blood? Why did He bother? After all He had left heaven for this world; why die as an outcast of the people?

We would like to think that the Jews and the Romans of Christ's time were responsible for the nails, but we were there, too. All of us had a part in the crucifixion. Since Christ is God as well as man, there was no future, no past; all of us were out there, taking a very real part on Calvary's hill. Did He perhaps see us detour to avoid Him when He called to us? Were we hurrying away to an easier life, one in which we would suffer less pain, less loneliness? The make-believe world of materialism had called to us. We refused to listen to His broken whisper, nor did we see the meaning of the sagging, broken Christ on a cross.

On that awful day, which saw the God of love nailed to a cross, were we running away? Did blood-filled eyes watch us hurry to quiet valleys where the meadows of wild flowers blew gently in the breeze? At that moment did the

God-Man's eyes fill with deep disappointment because we had not even thanked Him for the greatest gift He could give — a chance to love Him?

Why can we not say something like this? "Thank You, even though I do not like the pain life gives me, nor do I understand what I will do in the days to come. The future is so uncertain. Let me remember to carry with me a heart filled with gratitude all the days of my life for just the privilege of loving You."

We mustn't forget the God who died for us, and if we hear His voice asking us for something we treasure, we shouldn't refuse Him. A prayer of thanks must come from our hearts, even when our eyes are wet with tears. His is a love that will always shield us, if we only trust Him. We should be grateful for everything. Even pain and loneliness can bring us within reach of the comforting hand of an all-loving God.

4

Nobody Likes Me

When I was a young Sister I had a boy in my class whom I will call John Bradley. He wasn't an attractive child. His clothes indicated he was from a poor family, and he possessed an uncontrollable temper. If things did not go John's way he reacted by banging books, flinging his coat on a hook, or taking it out on something that was nearby. This always amused the other children and made them laugh, while it was a test of patience for me. Sometimes I would become very provoked and say sharply, "You pick up that book and put it down quietly!"

The year went past quickly, and almost before I knew it April arrived. The boys used to play baseball at recess time, but somehow John never got into the games. I had almost given up trying, for whenever I came upon the scene, John was alone — a drab little figure whom no one seemed to want to be bothered with. He became more isolated, more irritable as the days passed.

One day I went into my classroom after lunch to pick up some papers. I was about to go to the playground when John came in like a cyclone. "Bang!" went a book. The storm inside of him was raging full force. I said nothing — just waited and watched. Finally John arose, banged his book shut and stamped to the back of the room. His steps hammered angrily on the wooden floor, drowning out the usual squeak.

"John," I said, "what's wrong? Why are you crying?"

For a moment he couldn't speak. Finally he choked out the words: "Nobody likes me! *Nobody!*"

"Of course they do," I said. "I like you."

The tears were still streaming down John's face, and he seemed to look straight through me for a moment before saying, "Well, you're the only one."

There was a deep loneliness and hurt in his voice which I never forgot. How he longed for the recognition of classmates, for them to notice him, to ask him to join in their games. And because they rejected him he became more withdrawn, more difficult. To John at that moment I was the only one who liked him. It made me feel humble and small when I thought of the few times I had seen his eyes light up and a smile appear. This occurred when I asked him to do something for me, or praised him, or thanked him.

Rev. John Powell, S.J., has said in his book *Why Am I Afraid to Love?*, "Our lives are shaped by those who love us — by those who refuse to love us." John had been formed mostly be those who refused to love him. And somehow I wonder if we don't form more people around us by refusal than by love. Is our sin of not loving, the sin which we never consider wrong? I could have been much kinder to John. After all, it shouldn't have taken me until April to discover that his rejection was causing his displays of temper and violence. But, I am so dull at times, I have to fall over something before I see it.

Small wonder that we find abnormal behavior in a world that is more absorbed in material things than in people! We talk of clearing slums in a distant city while poor people all around us are starving for a kind word, or a smile, or a friendly gesture. We look over their heads and dream of a remote world where our deeds of love will shine like stars bringing light to the darkest corners, but there is never a thought of dispelling shadows in our own tiny yard. We forget our Lord's words: "Whatever you have done for the least of these, you have done for Me."

John's peers did not mean to be unkind. If I had chided them for not accepting him, one of the first excuses would have been: "But, Sister, I never do anything to him. I don't even touch him." And they would have been right in saying this — they just left him completely alone. They never harmed him physically. Instead they laughed at him and bruised his spirit and broke his heart, making him strike out at the whole world in the only way he knew how. They did not mean to hurt him, but hurt, unfortunately, does not depend upon intention.

Today, with the April sky a pale blue and lovely white clouds floating about, I wonder about all the John Bradleys of the world — the young, the old — the John Bradleys who are formed by those who refuse to love them. It takes so little to lift up a human heart. Yet we are so stingy.

We hoard kind, gentle words like a modern Midas hoards his gold. Pharisaically, we dream of doing great things for God while we ignore the people who are hungrily waiting and watching for someone to love them — someone to say: "I care and I am concerned about you." Kindliness waters the blooms which brighten the world. They grow by the wayside like wild flowers in springtime — forgotten except for a few nature lovers who generally also love God and man.

On the road to Calvary were there people who ignored Christ? Were some of those who saw Him completely absorbed in their own business? Oh, perhaps they were not bad, but just too busy to give Him any more than an idle glance of curiosity. After all, in those days of Roman subjugation, it was probably not an uncommon sight to see people forced to carry their own cross to the designated place of execution.

Veronica wasn't too busy though. She braved the crowd. She let the whole world know that she was a friend of this Man who was being struck and pushed and spat upon and screamed at by a vicious mob. Veronica forced her way through the crowd to wipe the blood and dirt from a face that had once been so beautiful and now was hardly recognizable. How the suffering Christ must have loved her for that act of kindness.

There are so many people on life's highways who need the sound of our voice, the touch of our hand to let them know that we love them. Yet, we lock ourselves in our own tired worlds, remembering only our own petty hurts, our own broken dreams. We forget in our day of turmoil, a day filled with the hollow sound of tinkling cymbals, that Christ can be found only in the love of our fellowman.

When the day of reckoning comes, will our hands be warm with the little unremembered acts of kindness? Or will we have only cold hands that did not really strike out at anyone, but that refused to give of their love for fear that they might be hurt in the giving? Will there be a John Bradley there to say, "Because of you I made it"? Will the God of love say as He once said to a heartbroken Magdalene: "Many sins are forgiven you because you have loved much"?

5

The Woman Who Begged

One of the Benedictine Sisters I live with has been a special friend of mine for a long time. She always listens to my hard-luck stories as if they were the most important thing in the world. Once in the spring when the air was still crisp and cold with a touch of winter still lingering in its wind, I came home from the mission where I was stationed feeling as if God had gone to the planet Mars for the duration.

We walked up and down a path with the wind blowing in our faces, and then against our backs. She listened to my problem sympathetically, knowing she could not solve it. It is usually impossible to solve other people's problems. But in a way she did solve it. She drew my attention to the Canaanite woman of our Lord's time. Evidently Christ was not paying much attention to her when she first started to beg. After thinking about it for a short time I shook off the shackles of disappointment and discouragement. Christ did not expect me to give up merely because He did not remove all obstacles in my path.

How vividly St. Matthew describes the pleadings of the Canaanite woman of Christ's time! In his Gospel he almost exposes the pain of her heart as she goes crying after the Lord. And how does He answer her? "It is not fair to take the children's bread and cast it to the dogs."

The words seem harsh, and very strange coming from the lips of the gentle Savior. Still the woman didn't give up, didn't turn away. Softly and humbly the words must have fallen from her lips, "Yes, Lord; for even the dogs eat of the crumbs that fall from their masters' table."

How the heart of Christ must have yearned in those far-away days to carry His message of love into pagan lands. Rome, Tyre, Sidon may have lingered in His thoughts, and haunted His dreams. Yet He confined Himself to Judea and Galilee. These were His people, a stiff-necked people, but nonetheless His people.

Why would God send His only begotten Son to a people who, as a whole, wanted no part of Him? They spurned His love and finally nailed Him to a cross. Was it to teach us by example that the only success is doing the right thing regardless of persons or places? This isn't an easy lesson to learn. It is hard, dreadfully hard, especially since we are so terribly human.

I have often wondered how Christ felt when He heard those He was dying to save clamoring for His death.

Since He was man as well as God, Christ cringed interiorly under the blows and wild, angry words hurled at Him, not only by the Roman soldiers, but by His own chosen people. In spite of everything His dry cracked lips did not utter words of anger or threat, but only love and forgiveness.

Sometimes the germ of discouragement clutches at our hearts. We would like to slip away from all worry and turmoil. We have become weary, our backs ache, the sun blazes, and there is no satisfaction in our work. How we would like more than anything else to feel the breeze of applause and love upon our faces.

No one would miss us if we slipped away; in fact they would not even know we were gone. We should not deceive ourselves — the King would miss us. And deep in our hearts we would know that we had not trusted Him, had not loved enough. Somehow we would always carry with us the awful feeling that we had failed Him. The whole world might be ours, but the whole world is not worth very much if it means giving up Christ.

Life is very short. The only thing that will remain when the door of death opens for us will be the little acts of unremembered charity performed in His name. Stars may shine brighter, birds may sing sweeter songs, and the whole world take on a brighter hue in other parts of the world, yet what difference does it really make? The Tyres and Sidons of our day may have a glamour all their own, yet we could accomplish very little in these places without His love.

When the soft tints have gone out of the sky, and the whole world seems a seething, helpless tangle of hopelessness we must remember that the Light of the world once hung on a rough cross. He was lonely, forsaken, yet He never gave up, never ceased doing His Father's will. We must kneel before Christ in the tabernacle of His love and beg Him to strengthen us when we want to run away from all that is hard and painful.

6

Locked Doors

The sun slid over the used-car parking lot, while the early spring wind skipped with a merry murmur through the open windows. The door of the seventh grade banged shut; the girls jumped, I sighed. When a girl tried to open the door, she couldn't because the lock had jammed. The decimals I was teaching bowed and were forgotten. Grasping the door knob, I tried to move it, but it refused to budge. I sighed again.

Behind me, the girls were making little delighted sounds. This was interesting, something that fascinated them far more than math problems. After discovering the keys to the room in a desk drawer, I tried to slide them under the door; there wasn't enough space. Since this attempt was futile, I gestured to a girl in the hall to get another key and a Sister teaching nearby. Sister came, and I could hear her trying to get the key to catch in the lock.

We went back to the decimals; at least I did. I noticed some of the girls waving and smiling. The girl at the board had her attention on what lay beyond the glass door. My head ached and I felt weary.

Linda's voice rose with little throbs of excitement. "Sister, isn't this fun! Maybe we'll be locked in all night.

Wouldn't it be nice?" Her face glowed with youthful anticipation.

I didn't think it would be, so I didn't answer. Locked doors are one of the things which make me uncomfortable. When I was a child and my mother went away, one of the chief weapons of my older sister was to threaten locking me in the cellar. If I pushed my luck too far, I found the inevitable happened. The cellar was dark and the smell of dampness was all about me. I was afraid of the dark. Perhaps this is where I acquired my phobia for locked doors.

Several moments later the door opened. We went slowly back to our neglected decimal points, but they were as dull as reading philosophy after watching a horse race.

It is easy to let the door of our lives bang shut on God. In the citadel of our own small minds we become absorbed in other matters. We can keep the door jammed for months and sometimes years. Oh, we console ourselves with the thought that we aren't too bad. We wouldn't think of missing Mass, of stealing, of lying, but we can become smug and selfish.

It is not so much what we do for Christ, but the love with which we do it. The God who commands legions of angels does not need our feeble efforts. He wants only our love.

It is possible to become niggardly in our spiritual life. When Christ tries to insert the key of love into our hearts, He finds the lock is jammed with strange pieces of selfishness, ambition, power and pride. There is some person we cannot like. In vain He tries to explain to our wayward hearts that love consists in wishing our neighbor the best. This tremendous God-Man tries His utmost to make it clear that He lives and moves and loves equally in this person (to whom we refuse to speak) as in us.

The lock does not click. We keep Him outside at a safe distance, fearing the demands He would make, once he gained a foothold, would be too high. How small we are in our relationship with God! We are struggling pygmies, seeking happiness in the deep jungles of our inner selves.

All the time Christ is searching through the swamps of a sin-laden world for us. He is once more carrying the heavy crossbeam on the way to Calvary, waiting for the sound of a voice that trusts and loves Him, even when He is covered with blood. Our God cringes under the blows of the soldiers. And we, to whom He has given all, go merrily on our way, refusing in our materialistic age to be bothered with anything so old-fashioned as love of a God who died for us centuries ago.

If only we would open the door of our hearts and let the fresh spring winds of God's love sweep through, how different we would be; how different the world would be! But you and I have let fear of human respect lock us in its cold, hard grasp.

We are afraid to be different. Instead of the soft voice of Christ in our hearts we hear the tread of social-conscious footsteps whose sharp, cruel pace causes us alarm and brings the icy look of fear into our eyes.

Unless we untangle ourselves from the clutches of the pleasure-mad world in which we live, we will never unlock doors. Nor shall we feel the touch of a wounded hand upon our hearts — a touch which will make us love the whole world in Him, through Him and with Him.

Perhaps we have tried to take the nails out of Christ's hands, making Him a convenient God. We have not succeeded. Love demands a *price,* and the proof of our love for Christ is letting Him become the unquestioned King of our hearts.

7

What Would Benedict Do?

Late in the afternoon I came back from a land of shadows to a world of reality to find myself in a hospital bed. Somewhere, I thought perhaps I dreamed it in the hammock of the night, I remembered falling, and the terrific pains in my ankle which followed the fall. A voice from the great beyond asked, "Are you awake enough to understand what I am saying?"

At that moment there was no desire in me to pluck memories from the ether and assemble them, so I dragged out a reluctant and muffled, "Yes." The voice went on: "Your ankle is broken in three places. The doctor thinks he will have to do an open reduction. It will be X-rayed tomorrow. You'd better pray. Sister pinned a St. Benedict medal on the cast. . . ."

But I had gone back to my world of shadows where all was pleasant. *Benedict!* The word stuck fast in my foggy mind. It was there when I awoke to find two nurses bending over the foot of the bed looking at an ankle which weighed me down like a ball and chain. They were moving their flashlight from side to side.

It was no surprise when the doctor told me the next day that the three bones were in perfect position. "This is very rare, and you are lucky," he had said. "It is seldom that you can set three bones without opening an ankle." It was no surprise because I somehow believed that St. Benedict helped.

Now with all the new words like commitment, involvement, dialogue, discussion, and the others which have been introduced into our perplexed society during the last decade, I keep wondering what Benedict would do and say if he lived in our times instead of the decaying era of the Romans.

It clutters up my mind at prayer, in school — everywhere. Would Benedict be a demonstrator, or a theorist with solutions to all problems? After all, the problems of mankind never change, only the attempted solutions.

And today with the rain dripping softly through the budding leaves, with the wind stirring the branches ever so slightly, I am beginning to think as perhaps Benedict thought the day he left Rome.

Around him was the goddess of pleasure, wearing a mask of charm while holding the people in her fond embrace. But Benedict, the Roman aristocrat, was not fooled. Perhaps people insisted that he could do much in Rome, that with all he had to offer it would be possible to alleviate human suffering. Yet when he was alone a voice whispered through the days and nights, "God — who else can help You help others?"

Benedict knew the futility of a mere human solution for a superhuman problem. He knew that he must help the soul in order to really help the tired, hungry and poor who crouched defensively in the sunshine of the streets. He knew, too, that help without love is dust.

With a knowledge beyond his years he fled from Rome — not because he was afraid of life, but rather because he had a rendezvous with the God who would teach him how to help. The hillside of Subiaco was lonely. As he watched the stars come into the sky at night he found it easy to remember, but hard to forget the people he loved. Temptations taunted him, reaching out to him with enticing fingers, when his whole spirit seemed plunged in a dungeon of darkness.

He remembered candlelight shining warmly on white linens, and the gleam of silver. He was young, with a haunting loneliness for loved ones. People he had left behind played hopscotch over half-forgotten memories. Benedict fought all this, not with the mind of a Stoic, but with the determination to meet and know the God of love in this wild solitude.

Then after some time, when Benedict had won the fight, and the peace of God had taken possession of him, the poor shepherds of the valleys came trudging up the hillside to him. The word got around very fast, even in those times, that this man was different; he gave them help by giving them peace — he gave them peace by giving them God. They came bringing with them their poor, their crippled, their heartbroken.

Those who had lost hope had it restored, while the sorrowful went away comforted. Even the worldly wise from Rome found their way to Benedict's feet, opening the doors of a Bluebeard's chamber of hidden anxiety to him. They went away realizing that this was not an impractical dreamer who had fled from responsibility, but one who had found the key to solve their problems.

The spirit of St. Benedict is still alive in our day. It is a gentle spirit, one that brings peace to tired hearts and minds. It stands on lonely mountainsides, in quiet valleys, in cities and villages — everywhere that people are to be found. But we never can find it unless we take time out to find God.

We must remember in our harassed times that the "heresy of good works" may become an obstacle to reaching the God of heaven who once said, "Without Me you can do nothing." We must reach out to Him, and beg Him to keep us from becoming so absorbed in work that we forget there were the "hidden" years in Christ's life when He heard only the sound of the saw in a carpenter shop, and the thud of the sledge. Then there was a brief three years of public life, ending with the Son of God dying on a lonely cross, unknown to most of mankind. Without God good works alone have the foundation of shifting sand.

8

We Should Trust Him

The pastor and I were in the midst of a conversation when a soft whisper startled us. "Father, look what I did!"

The blue eyes raised to the priest were full of confidence. Then I saw. Blood was streaming from the foot of the tiny flaxen-haired girl. Father quickly seated her in a chair and went for the car keys while I tried to stop the bleeding. Her leg trembled, but when I asked, "How did you do this, honey?" the voice was still soft, like the wind blowing over the meadows in springtime. "I don't know. I turned my foot, and looked down, and it was bleeding."

A fifth-grade boy dashed in late for instructions. I did not look up, but I heard his frightened voice, "What happened?" Before I had time to answer, he had hurried away.

Just as I had finished tying my handkerchief around the tiny foot, Father was back with the car keys. Since he was carrying Nita, I went out to the car to open the door. Again there was the look of trust. She sat straight and quiet in the front seat where she scintillated with charm.

Now all week, even when everything went wrong, the picture of a little girl's faith in Father played leapfrog through the rooms of my restless memory. It was a stimulus more powerful than drugs — a haunting impression demanding an audience in my spiritual life.

In our day of riots, mass killings, strikes and all the other happenings which tend to clutter up our lives with a wild terrified fear, we are apt to develop a neurotic secondhand sort of spirituality. God becomes something we cling to hysterically in this nightmare of change, but we begin after a time, to doubt His power to help. We have forgotten that He is the God of Hosts. However, slowly memory comes back of what He said to Peter, who in his haste struck off the ear of Malchus that eventful night when even the air about Christ was heavy with the power of evil: "Do you not think that I could ask My Father for twelve legions of angels, and He would give them to Me?"

He whispers the same power-laden words in our day. In the garden that night everything seemed lost, and Christ Himself seemed to be a contradiction which left minds like Peter's gasping for a breath of faith. Peter always builds up my morale, because he, too, lacked trust. I wonder if the words of Christ ever reached the excited mind of Peter.

But I have digressed from Nita and her perfect trust.

The greatest compliment we can pay Christ is to trust Him on the darkest days of our lives when we do not know the way. The answers to our puzzling questions play a confusing game of hide-and-seek. Even in crowds we feel alone and lost like an ageless Robinson Crusoe on a desert island. At times we try to go through life without the mighty help of the Redeemer, but suddenly the storms become wild and furious. It is then we must call to Him through the darkness: "Lord, save us. We perish." But we are so slow to trust Him. Our confidence flickers like a dying candle in the night, then slowly goes out, if we are not careful.

All of us have a work which we shall do or it will remain undone for eternity. In our shadowland we must search through the gloom, listening intently for the voice which says, "Come to Me." This will not always be easy, for when our souls are weary with the struggles of life, and our hearts are bleeding with misunderstanding, it is difficult to trust.

Maybe, if we were to spend some time in each day kneeling before the God of love in the Blessed Sacrament, we would be different. We could talk to Christ as Nita did to Father, and know that there is nothing to fear as long as He is with us. I think that is perfect trust. Our prayer might be like this:

"It is hard, Lord, to trust You when all about me there is hate and distrust. I wanted to spend my life in the quiet of Bethlehem's cave, but You set me in a field where everything seems strife and confusion. I am puzzled and often I do not understand. I am weak, and You are strong. Temptations and anxieties are all about me in every form. Yet I will always trust You, regardless of the darkness. I know You meant it when You said, 'Behold, I am with you always.'"

9

Are We Indifferent to Others?

Just before I went into the study hall that early May morning, my attention was attracted by a notice on the bulletin board. It read: "No one is to leave any of the rooms the first period this morning."

Although I never left the room during the first period, I decided today I would just be different. If only I hadn't seen that notice — but I had, and now my mind was working fast. I opened my book, looked down at the French verbs, chewed the end of my pencil, and pretended to study. Around me pages turned, feet moved restlessly, while a robin on a branch of the tree near the window sang a joyous song.

I looked up and watched Miss Walters. She would have made an excellent picture for a spinster club — tall, slight, hair combed straight back, with a very plain dress, and as usual an uninterested face. Now my plan was to go into effect. I pushed my book aside, arose from my seat, and walked up to Miss Walters. Feigning embarrassment I coughed, then asked, "May I please go out and get my handkerchief in my coat pocket?"

She turned, gave me a quick look, then nodded her head in an impersonal manner.

A few pairs of eyes looked at me in surprise as I walked past. Inside of me, there were feeble notes of triumph. In spite of the notice about not leaving the room, I had permission to do just that. It was then that I almost collided with Mr. Connelly, my freshman homeroom teacher. He wasn't happy about meeting me, and he knew me very well.

"Didn't you see the bulletin board?" he asked, then added quickly, as the truth dawned on him, "Oh, I see, just because it said you weren't to leave the room, you are going to. I have never seen anyone like you. You — " He stopped abruptly.

Out of the corner of my eye I saw Miss Walters slowly walking down the aisle. When she spoke, her voice was completely devoid of the spring sounds which were drifting through the windows. "Mr. Connelly, I'll attend to this!"

By the time I reached the cloakroom I felt small and cheap. I really hadn't bargained for this. It wasn't because I wanted to create a feud between the two teachers. I only wanted to. . . . There my thoughts failed me. Why had I planned all this in the first place? What had I accomplished? The answer was there flooding my teen-age mind. I had really played a childish game of pretense with an unhappy ending.

Even as adults we retain that same childish characteristic by forgetting about God when we plan something. At the time we think it is a great idea, and then we find ourselves face-to-face with chagrin and doubt. Life is always a mystery, and why we want to do the things we are not to do is even puzzling to ourselves. God's commandment is simply to love Him and our neighbor. However, the doing is not as simple as the saying. Our lives speak like this for the greater part: "To love You, God, is easy. Sure, I love You. Don't I go to Holy Communion once a month? Doesn't all this prove that I love You?

"But my neighbor — well, that's another story. How can I love the man down the street who borrows my lawn mower and never returns it? How can I love my sister-in-law, who is exacting and makes me wish she would go to some distant planet and never come back?"

We could go on and on with enough material to fill books. But we are only playing a little game of adolescent spirituality. We are hiding the real reason why we aren't better men and women. It is impossible to make the world and the people with whom we come in contact as we would like them to be. We cannot dress them up to suit our whims and desires. They are there with all their faults and failings and we must accept them. Easy? No, it is dreadfully hard at times.

But what about God: do we really love Him? Does Good Friday mean anything to us, or is it just a date on the calendar? Do we just go our merry way, never being very good or really bad? Somehow, I think we do. We dream our own personal dreams in which the Son of God never enters. Christ is a far-away God-Man, belonging to a different century, a different world. It is easy, if we aren't careful, to become self-satisfied with our mediocre life. Christ doesn't have a big part in it, for we give Him only the crumbs that fall from our table.

If Christ walked the streets of our towns and villages today, what would He think? Would He feel like a stranger on our highways, in our streets? Would the poem *Indifference* describe it?

> . . . When Jesus comes to modern towns,
> They simply pass Him by;
> They do not hurt a hair of Him.

They only let Him die.
For men have grown more tender;
And would not give Him pain.
They only pass Him down the street;
And leave Him in the rain. . . .

Are we perhaps rushing to eternity without a thought of those with whom we come in contact every day? Someone on life's journey is waiting for the sympathy which we can give, the glad smile, or just the cheery "hello." It is not the great deeds we perform that will be our passport to heaven, but only the little kindnesses we show to others each day.

10

First Things First

A sudden thought occurred to me while I was sitting in the doctor's office. There was an awkward pause, and my wording was like that of a schoolgirl hurrying over a difficult lesson, afraid that she would be questioned about it: "Doctor, I gave blood. Was it all right?"

Perhaps another doctor would have told me flatly that one does not ask for approval for something already done, but the doctor who checks me periodically didn't, even though he had every right to be annoyed.

"Sister," he replied courteously, although a bit dryly, "it was all right, but you shouldn't have done it. There you go trying to be a 'do-gooder.' "

"It really makes me feel better," I said quickly.

A smile spread over his face as he asked: "How? Spiritually?"

Telling him that it made me feel better physically was a lost cause. But I did anyway, even though the remark now seems to have been rather immature.

Just the same, the "do-gooder" business became tangled in my mind and refused to leave even after I had left the doctor's office and mingled once again with the ordinary things in life. I kept wondering and thinking about people in general today. Are they so absorbed in doing good that they forget the Author of goodness?

We can easily apply a textbook spirituality to our lives, even making ourselves believe that we are doing much good in the world about us. If we are not careful the line will snag and our artificial bait will be lost in the murky water of humanitarianism.

In our eagerness for "do-gooding" we whitewash our hearts with a deluge of superficial activity for mere activity's sake. We become alarmed at what we see and hear about us and wish to become do-gooders, proving our worth to the world by becoming absorbed in it. For a long, long time we delude ourselves into thinking that the world had lost its significance, and now we wish to save it by forcing our do-gooder deeds upon it.

A do-gooder is like a bird that no longer sings except when all the world is watching. Life has lost its meaning for that person, and has left its stigma of discontent upon the face and heart. He cannot give to others a love that is like a robin singing in the rain, bringing joy to those who no longer see the sun, nor feel its warmth upon their hearts. A person like this cannot give to others a joy which he himself does not possess. And he becomes, without knowing it, a pretender.

In our day of riots, change and rumblings of war, we forget that we are Christians following a God who let Himself be taken and nailed to the rough wood of the cross that we might live our lives in peace, knowing that someday we will be united with Him. We look for ways and means to salve our troubled conscience and sometimes come up with the answer that to be a do-gooder is all we need — but is it?

Can we really help the world if we neglect the God who died for us to serve those lesser gods who play havoc with our hearts? Should it happen that we neglect to love the God of heaven, we will find ourselves trying to play a magical music of spirituality upon a tin horn. The sounds that come forth will be harsh with discord. We will never win the world for Christ unless we love Him first. The real love we should bestow is an art which only God can teach us.

Do-gooders are not the answer to our noisy, heartbreaking world, but those who feel the wind of another world blowing over their faces are, for they have learned the art of loving. They have looked through a haze of blood and recognized the God of heaven in the horribly bruised face of humanity.

He who alone knew the solution to the mystery of life said: "Thou shalt love the Lord thy God with thy whole heart, and with thy whole soul, and with thy whole mind. This is the greatest and the first commandment. And the second is like it: Thou shalt love thy neighbor as thyself" (Mt. 22:37-39).

It seems sophomoric to attempt the second precept before the first has been achieved. Yet in our haste to bind up a world that is suffering from the wounds of hate, we forget that His love must be the beginning of all things. If we forget to put it first, we are merely flirting with folly.

11

Fishing Days — Dreaming Days

After the snow has melted and the sun has dried the little puddles of slushy water the real magic of spring appears. There is something in me that leaps up and wants to go to a place where memories hide by the side of a stream, where quiet winds blow all the meaningless formalities of civilization from my mind. There would be no puzzled faces of children struggling in a morass of math problems — children who wish to turn me off but cannot. But since this place is miles and years away I can only dream of it, and thank God for the joy He gave me there.

When the birds began to sing and the Mayflowers and violets had lifted their heads from their winter pillow, when the music of the wind was sweet and low, the untamed part of me used to come alive. Then I would go fishing. You really couldn't call it fishing though, because I was too squirmy to even take a fish off a hook. My brothers did it for me.

Oh, they teased me about it, but they were too good-natured to tell me I should get over this. Besides, they figured that girls are supposed to act that way. But there was a time in spring when I wanted to go fishing alone. I used to wear one of Joe's shirts. (Why I took it I don't know, since it was sizes too large.) Then I would take one of Ed's fishing poles and off I would go. I never was perturbed about the bait because I wasn't really interested in catching fish.

Along the stream I would leisurely walk, dangling the line in a way which would have caused a real fisherman to shudder, or laugh, depending on his disposition. Anyway, I got a lot of joy out of this. I felt free with the sun shining on my face and the wind blowing through my hair. The whole world seemed bright. When I found a pleasant spot, I would sit on the grass and watch the water run over moss-covered rocks and listen to all the sounds of nature, and dream . . . dream . . . dream. Perhaps it wasn't very practical for a fourteen- or fifteen-year-old girl to do this, but then I have never been a practical person.

It wasn't that I didn't like people — I could usually strike up a conversation with a perfect stranger very quickly and easily. It was just that I wanted to get away from the humdrum world for just a little while. Was it a deficiency in my natural makeup that had to be supplied by the out-of-doors?

Often I have thought how wonderful it would be to go back to those idyllic days for just one hour, but I know it could never be the same. Somebody once wrote a book with the title *You Can't Go Home*. Now that I am a Benedictine nun and have not returned to my childhood environment for such a long, long time the people I knew would somehow disturb me. "Do you remember when you . . . ?" they would ask, as they did when I went to my father's and Ed's funerals. I love these people; yet those who were nearest and dearest to me are dead or gone. My mother wouldn't be there to say when I had forgotten someone's name, "You remember Mrs. Starks!" No, it would be a different world now.

So each spring I take out these memories as a miser does his gold from a chest. I fondle them, examine them, then lock them once more in the treasure room of my heart. They are the laughter and song of another age, a time of apple blossoms and the sound of a breeze murmuring through the green grass on the edge of a stream.

Life at that time was simple. I did not peer anxiously into the future wondering if God would provide, if He would always be there for me to lean on. He had given me health and love. What more did I need to be happy? No one said, "The way things are going you don't know what's going to happen." There was just one day at a time to be lived — no anxious searching into the future, no wondering if all the dreams that were dreamed would become hollow and broken. Oh, everyone had problems and troubles, but they accepted them, and learned to live with them and didn't seem to feel sorry for themselves.

In recent years I sometimes wonder if the rust of winter snows and cold rains have made bleak paths upon my mind and heart. Have I perhaps lost my trust in the providence of God? Have I become so involved in the modern jargon of identity, commitment, and relevant apostolate that I forget there is a world of sunshine and rainbows and spring winds waiting for me?

Not long ago a man said to me, "Sister, you're a dreamer," and I stared at him, puzzled. I had talked to him about his daughter, about books, about many things, but certainly not about my dreams. After all, I wasn't that naive. However, he had read my book. In it perhaps he had discovered that there was something I hadn't surrendered when I entered religious life — my dreams!

We are so afraid of being considered different; so afraid that people will consider us "square"; so afraid to think our own spiritual thoughts. In fact, we are so concerned about impressing people that He who said, "Knock and it shall be opened to you," could knock day and night at the door of our hearts, and it would remain forever closed to Him. He is not even permitted to sit on the doorstep for fear of what the neighbors might think.

When I go back to those spring days I cannot remember being worried about what the neighbors would think. They accepted me just as I was, and I loved them. I laughed when Steve Chilton would say: "You didn't catch any fish, did you? Isn't that Ed's fishing pole?" The answers to both questions were quite apparent. Neither did my youthful cavorting bother Mrs. Longtin who suffered from arthritis. She would come out on her porch and call to me, "I just baked a pie. Come in and have a piece with me."

And I would go into her immaculate house, leaving the pole on the porch. We would enjoy the pie. She never said a word about fishing. She liked having me, and I liked being with her. Yet neither Steve nor Mrs. Longtin ever tried to look into the keyhole of my heart, to figure out why I did things. The very thought of those people who taught me so much about life and love makes me feel warm and grateful.

Love to me is a simple thing. It is a teasing voice in the midst of a drab day. It is the thoughtful word someone is not too hurried to say. It is in the eyes of a child who needs you. Sometimes it is only the expression of concern for your worries on a friend's face, or a smile. Yes, love is made up of little things. Why have we made it such a complicated art? The slums, the inner city have always been all around us. Slums and inner city are not modern inventions. Christ knew them well. "The poor you shall always have with you." We don't have to go peeking into the keyhole of human hearts in order to love them.

It is strange how we dream of doing great things for God and at the same time unappreciatively trample the Mayflowers and violets of spring. We continue our futile dream of building utopian gardens for the world. We forget that the real loveliness of God grows close to the soil, that we must be humble enough to stoop or we will never discover the treasures that another heart holds.

I always want to keep those first primary lessons of love intact. I want to remember the people of my early adolescent days in all their lovable simplicity. At my time in life I often wonder if James Russell Lowell was thinking of me when he wrote:

As life runs on, the road grows strange
With faces new, and near the end
The milestones into headstones change,
'Neath every one a friend.

12

Is God Dead?

When I first saw the cemetery outside of the window of the classroom where I taught last year I was unduly depressed. I was visiting there when I looked out of the window and caught a glimpse of its vastness. I said, "If I ever was sent here I would just die. Having to look at that cemetery every school day would kill me."

Now, to make a long story short, I was sent there. In fact, I learned to love that cemetery. If I wanted to really concentrate on anything I had to take it to the convent or go to the library which had no windows. Otherwise, I found myself sitting at my desk fiddling with a pencil or some other object and gazing at the peace and quiet I thought would kill me.

In the spring and fall I often took my spiritual reading there, walking up and down before the huge granite crucifix with its haunting sorrowful expression.

Even in the last days of winter the cemetery has a charm all its own. The trees are gaunt and somber against a gray sky; the tombstones are scrubbed clean and white by the storms of winter. Some of the graves have flags that are torn to shreds by the winter winds, while the artificial flowers that have been there a long time look faded.

On Memorial Day, when the field Mass takes place beneath the huge crucifix, everything comes alive again. There is a hushed silence, new flags flutter from the graves, flowers splash their color almost everywhere. The wind blows softly through the trees, and here and there a bird sings joyfully over the somber stones marking the graves of the ancient dead.

But the people who are buried there, those who have gone into eternity, what would they say if they spoke to us today? Once they knelt in church, fought their own personal battles, had their own dreams, and lived their lives just as those who are with us today. If they spoke to us, what would they say?

Would they tell us what they would do if they had a chance to live their lives over again? Would they tell us what it is like to cross from life here on earth into eternity? Somehow I think they would take us by the hand and show us the greatest Lover who walked the earth, giving of His love and never asking a return.

I think they would tell us that as the days slip past, the only important things in life are the little unremembered acts of kindness done in His name. These are the treasures that will gather no dust, nor will they ever rust or grow old and musty.

Once a little preschool girl named Jean Marie was brought to the library to see me. She sat in a chair directly across from me, swung her legs back and forth and studied me with lovely blue eyes. Finally she asked, "Is God really dead?"

I put the book I was mending down in amazement and replied, "Of course not. Who told you that?"

She leaned across the table and whispered in an awed voice, "I know He is dead. I saw Him."

"Now where did you see Him? I never saw God."

"In the cemetery," she replied confidentially. "I saw Him hanging on that big stone cross in the cemetery."

It wasn't easy to explain to Jean Marie and I'm not sure she understood that God was very much alive. It would have been impossible to tell her that He still watches over the weary world. Yet there are many adults who are so puzzled as this little girl with the wide bright eyes.

I remember a desk at St. Bonaventure University on which was carved: "God is dead." Below it in sharp contrast was: "My God is alive; too bad about yours."

What message would those people who are buried there give us today? Somehow I think they would tell us above all else that God is very much alive. They would whisper to our aching hearts that the sun will someday shine again, and the streams splash over jagged rocks when once more laughter returns to the world as God lives more fully in our hearts. They would tell us not to be discouraged when a thousand distressed butterflies with broken wings flutter within us and do not seem able to find an exit.

There is so much I think the dead would tell us about God's mercy and love. But in our wild world, where love has become a byword without meaning, we are intoxicated with the artificial works of time. It is so much easier now to stay alive, but far more difficult to be a human being.

We demand that others love us, forgetting that we cannot force the door of anyone's heart to open to us. We have become empty of hope. We no longer seem to realize that we can only live in Christ and for Christ or we do not live at all. There is no other way for a Christian.

In our rush to get things done, is God's voice becoming feeble? Is His calm, His joy buried under a dying heap of "relevant" works that are meaningless? Have we all but forgotten that there is Someone waiting to love us in time and eternity?

How often, sitting at my desk, chewing the end of my pencil, I have thought of the dead in that cemetery and other people who have lived and loved and died and who have gone before us! How often I have wondered if they saw the horribly bruised Christ in struggling human beings!

People lost heart at Calvary. They wanted perhaps to flee to the hills where they would never again have to view a crucifixion. And they were frightened — terribly frightened and puzzled. How mysterious life can be at times when the burning and flaming sky blur into one and we are not sure of anything.

God: how the Word should be burned into our hearts! Eternity is so near to all of us, and yet we feel the cold, still fingers of the world reaching out and touching our hearts, placing a chill upon them, a strange foreboding we cannot dispel. Yet, if we had more faith and love, this would never interfere with our loyalty to God who has His being deep within the recess of our human hearts. How real He is; how loving and understanding!

Yet you and I forget all this and tremble and worry about the turmoil about us, letting it become part of us. It is so easy to forget when the clouds hang low, and understanding is but a word, that He is still there listening, waiting for us to love Him. We do seem to act and think as though God were dead. He is very much alive even though He is hanging on a stone cross in our cemetery. He will always be there for the weak who need Him.

II

Summer

*The woods were made for the
hunter of dreams,
The brooks for the fishers
of song.*

— Sam Walter Foss

1

Summer Sunlight and Storms

Standing at the door of an empty classroom just before handing in my keys at the end of a school year always gives me a peculiar feeling. Mentally I briefly check everything (records, desk, cupboard, etc.), knowing the school year is behind me forever.

If the class I have taught has been hard to manage, it moves grotesquely in a swollen dulled confusion through the tired chambers of my mind, and I lock the door quickly, then hurry away from the memories creeping in the summer heat. On the other hand, if it has been a good year, where I seem to have made some progress, I am reluctant to leave, to plunge into the heat and strife of summer. The temptation of fear is strong upon me — fear of the unknown.

Summer has come, and spring is at an end. It has slipped from my grasp, and I have no power to hold it even if I wanted to. Yet, I should remember my heart is free. No one, or nothing, can take from me the Spirit of God who dwells within me. This should be enough to keep me always young and optimistic regardless of what I may think the future holds.

But you and I forget all this as we peer into the future. We think of the angry storms with their thunder and lightning, of the humid nights and stifling days. Somehow we tend to grow old and cynical instead of wise and mellowed. It is so easy to lose our nerve, to forget that Christ is with us in the wild storms and blistering heat of summer.

The God-Man who let Himself be taken by His enemies and nailed to a cross cannot and will not fail us now. As the old song goes: "Prayer is the key to heaven but faith unlocks the door."

In our world of change and shifting shadows, where everything old has ceased to be "lavender and old lace" but has become a form of mold and mildew, we lose our trust in the God of heaven and earth, and our weary minds begin to wonder if it is worth it all. Discouragement plows a path through our hearts, burying all the flowers of hope that once bloomed there. Our shoulders slump, and we forget the strength of Christ and His love. Our dreams are gone, and in their place is a shallow practicality which runs helter-skelter over our spiritual life.

Like little Red Riding Hood in the old fairy tale, who looked at the wolf posing as her grandmother and remarked about the change in physical appearance of one she loved, we gaze at the people around us and begin to doubt and wonder. The eyes of the world seem huge and strangely devoid of interest. They seem to have lost their sense of direction in a maze of material obstacles. Many of us have lost our feeling of wonder and have become old and tired before our time. It should not be this way, only it is, apparently. We reach out longingly for something from the springtime of life — something that is old and familiar; yet, it becomes nothingness when we try to grasp it.

Hopeless as our surroundings may appear, the God of love is still in our lives. He is in the tabernacles of the world waiting for us. He whispers His song of joy to us when the wind blows through the very topmost branches of the trees — when the sun has set, the twilight is descending upon us in a hushed silence. His glory is in the sky where a rising sun paints its tints of delicate pink. But most of all He is in our hearts. Why should we let ourselves be afraid of what is to come — of wars, and riots, and murders? Horrible as these are, they can never destroy the Spirit of God who dwells within us. In our time it is so very easy to let the ghost of fear settle upon our lives, mangling our peace until it ceases to exist.

God never meant us to be unhappy, even when pain descends upon us in various forms. He meant us to lift our hearts to Him always and feel secure in the fact that He will always be there when we need Him. It is impossible perhaps to remove all anxiety from our lives because of the times in which we live. In spite of all the darkness about us we must go on trusting. Someday, somehow, the stars will shine again in a glittering sky, and we shall know the joy of being free.

Didn't the disciples feel on the road to Emmaus that everything was hopeless? St. Luke says they were conversing and arguing together, which leads us to believe that they did not always understand each other. They did not recognize Christ until the breaking of the bread. I keep wondering today if they felt as we do in our time — puzzled, bewildered, doubting, yet knowing definitely that the springtime of their life with Christ had passed. The three years were gone, and now they were no longer sure. The words, "But we were hoping that it was He who should redeem Israel," lead one to think their trust was beginning to wane. Christ finally revealed Himself to them, and in so doing once more lit the torch of hope within their hearts. Remember that these men knew Christ intimately.

They had listened to Him, felt the power that went out from Him and yet . . . they knew He had died on the cross. They had been His friends and now they were puzzled and confused. At the time when it seemed that they needed Him most, Christ came to them, reassuring them, leaving their hearts light with the knowledge that He was still with them, still loved them.

We have never seen Christ, never talked to Him in person. Our knowledge of Him has to be gathered through the Gospels which He left us. When we fear the summer of life and wonder where He has gone, we must keep the song in our hearts alive with the thought that He will never leave us. He alone has the power to light up the dark places of our lives with His presence. Only we must never stop searching for Him regardless of how dry and lifeless our days become.

2

A Strange Gift

As I sat on the porch of the guest house conversing with my mother, she suddenly said, "I lost my comb. I've had it for years."

"Comb?" I questioned.

Mother sighed, "Yes, the one you bought me when you were small and spent all the money you had — a dime or a quarter for it."

I laughed. But mother was wrapped in memories of the past, so I joined her.

My older sister and I were in the store which was set up especially for people who did not have all kinds of coins jingling in their pockets. I was clutching my entire wealth in a perspiring fist.

"Why don't you buy a picture book?" my sister asked. "I'd give you the extra money."

I shook my head. "No, I have to buy Mama a present."

"With a dime? You can't get anything she'd like with a dime!"

This time I didn't answer. At the age of five or six I was already showing signs of stubbornness. Standing on tiptoe, I looked over all the inexpensive items. And then I saw it—the black comb. "It's just what Mama needs!" I said.

"She doesn't need a comb!" my sister informed me, then stood in disapproving silence.

Finally she got me back to the car. I clutched my brown bag and sighed happily. As we drove along I tapped the toes of my patent leather shoes and watched the scenery. A few times I opened the bag, took out the comb and admired it. When the car stopped I did not wait for my sister, but ran up the driveway and into the house. My mother was in the kitchen bending over a hot stove. Running to her I handed her my precious gift saying, "I brought you something." Then I stood back, waiting for her reaction.

Immediately mother took me into her arms, telling me what a thoughtful child I was. After that I went upstairs, changed into my old clothes and went to the brook to wade.

The sun was shining through the trees. The moss-covered rocks felt soft beneath my feet. I listened to the song of the water as it played its magic music. I skidded flat stones over the smooth surface of the brook, watching as they disturbed the little pools of sunshine on the water. Before the sun had gone into hiding behind the hills, the comb had slipped away into my crowded land of memories.

Perhaps our meeting with Christ will be filled with half-forgotten deeds which will decide our place in eternity. Will there be little acts of kindness we no longer remember? Will there be smiles and understanding words given to someone whose heart was heavy with pain — perhaps someone who will be there to greet us when the day of life is done?

What will the God of love consider the most outstanding work we have done for Him? Will it be some great accomplishment in life that left people gasping in wonder, awe and admiration? If this is all, I fear we will not have much to offer.

In this age of hurrying through everything, we forget the tiny happenings on earth that make life worth living. Some of us have developed a craving for a manicured spirituality — one perfectly groomed and easily come by.

Nevertheless, our nearness to God does not consist in great deeds, but merely in our looking for Christ in the stranger, the orphan, the lost. We must peer through the mist until we find the lovable Christ hidden deep within our neighbor.

But we want to become spiritual giants before we have learned to walk in the humble paths Christ trod. It frightens us to think we would have to stroll through a meadow wild with June buttercups and pink clover, searching in the hot sunlight for the insignificant things which no one bothers about. We do not want to feel the heat of noonday, nor the chill of a cold winter wind.

In our exploring the moon and planets we are constantly looking skyward for we know not what, yet never see the stars. All our lives are spent searching for an illusory distant loveliness while we stumble over the beauty at our feet. Why are we blind to omnipresent wonders of God? Why have we forgotten the little things? Why must it be considered plebeian to admire the good that lies so near?

Perhaps in our search for happiness we have ignored the little things in life. We have forgotten the violets that grow close to the ground and have trampled them in our hurry to reach out for the bigger things in life.

3

Little Men in the Mountains

It was a hot afternoon in midsummer, somewhere in the beginning of my life, a time when my imaginative mind played games with the fairy tales and stories I had heard. To tell me a story, or read one, was an effective way of keeping me quiet, so I had heard many of them.

Now I gazed at the distant purple of the Adirondack Mountains as I sat alone eating an apple which should have remained on the tree a much longer time. I thought for a while about Washington Irving and his tale of the little men who lived in the mountains. Before long I found myself fastening strings to the little men and was making them do my bidding.

After a time I went into the house and startled everyone by saying, "There are little men who live up in those mountains."

My practical mother exclaimed, "What?"

Ed lowered his paper, gave me a startled look, then broke into an amused grin. "You tell lies," Paul, who was four years my senior, informed me.

"I wish you wouldn't tell her all those stories. You know she believes everything you tell her," mother said wearily.

It was then that I started to cry. "But there are little men there," I said stubbornly. "There are...."

It is not uncommon in adult life for our imagination to run wild. Often we try to pierce the purple haze of the future, or we create all kinds of lives for ourselves. We draw blueprints of our plans, placing people with whom we would most like to be in those plans. We dream dreams and, like children, do not wish anyone to tell us that they are impractical. We do not even want God to show us in any way that these powder-covered dreams are mere fantasies. If they materialize at all, they will perhaps bring upon us a perfect boredom in a few short years. On the other hand, we should never stop dreaming and thinking and hoping.

As a child I had no idea what was in or on those mountains, so I put something there that would suit my fancy, something that would appeal to me.

We have no idea of what the future holds for us, but we would like to arrange it in our own way. We do know that God has said He will be always with us. This should be enough for us. However, as soon as we look through the mist of the future and see the outlines of failure and disappointment we are frightened. We begin to depend on our own spiritual strength, which isn't very great, and we grow discouraged. We feel God has not given us what we really deserve. Our mind may even be gripped with the iron finger of fear, and life becomes a dull anguish without the anesthesia of tears.

We may become so absorbed in the material things of life that we fail to let Christ do the planning and arranging for us. We feel that we would like to take the whole plan from His hands and put it into a setting of our own choosing.

It is impossible to show God our love when our lives

are all ablaze with joy and sunshine. We prove it only when the smoke of battle fills our nostrils, and our whole being wants to withdraw to something which is easier and far less taxing. It isn't hard to love when the paths ahead of us are easy and straight.

There were many fair-weather friends who turned against Christ that first Good Friday. Some could not bear the sight of the twisted, tortured and bruised face of the Son of God, nor could they stand the sight of those eyes which looked down upon them through a film of blood. That is why many fled Calvary that day. They are still doing it in our day.

The cross of Christ has never been attractive. Even though suffering has a thousand faces, not one has any appeal. The Blessed Mother and the few faithful people who remained on Calvary did not really consider the cross; they were looking at the Figure on the cross.

The reason why we fear sufferings and turn into moral cowards is that we look at life as something made up of all the trivial happenings that obstruct our path each day. It is quite easy to forget that life is not something but Someone. When we have become aware of this, writing it on our minds and hearts with indelible ink, we shall have reached the purple mountaintop where all is joy, for we shall have become immersed in the fact that He loves us.

4

Mike Swore

It was the middle of a hot afternoon when I walked into the pantry. Mother was baking cookies, and had just removed a pan from the oven. I reached over and took one with a feeling of elation. She was busy and had forgotten to say the usual, "You've been playing with the dog; wash your hands." But the cookie wasn't the real reason I had come indoors. I had news, big news — at least I thought it was.

I climbed up on a stool, dangled my feet, and said simply, "Mike swore." Mike imbibed too much and used strong language. Although I was afraid of him, I stood a short distance away and listened gleefully. Anyway it was pretty bad, and I wanted to know what Mother would say. My tongue was itching to repeat the words, and my childish mind told me that it would be no sin if Mother would only ask, "What did he say?" But Mother didn't utter a word, just went on cutting cookies as if she hadn't heard. Evidently she had a pretty good idea what Mike would say. I swallowed the bite of cookie and said in a louder tone, "Mike swore. He swore a whole lot."

The cookie cutter paused. Mother turned and looked at me as if she hadn't noticed me before, then said quietly,

"You pray for Mike." With that, she turned her attention back to the cookie cutter.

This was a disappointing reply. It was like a pail of cold water aimed at my impishness. Suddenly the green apples on a tree outside the window caught my attention, so I slid off my perch and left.

Strange how all that comes back to me today when I watch the Mikes around me — wanting to help but knowing that often my words will be rejected, regarded as either impractical or pietistic. How real and full of wisdom are those words, "You pray for Mike," now that I find myself standing on the edge of a vast world that is lonely and tries to fill its emptiness with pleasure. It is sad and seeks to bring joy into its life with forced laughter that is often empty and indifferent; it is unhappy because it has exchanged the God of love for the "golden image" of wealth and power. It begs for understanding and it forgets all about praying to God for what it needs. The world we live in tries to solve its problems by hurrying from one activity to another, while its futile attempts resemble those of the ants described so humorously by Mark Twain in his story *The Fraudulent Ant*.

We live in a society which is constantly changing, one that seems to have the imprint of restlessness upon it. We think we have to do great things for God, and lose sight of the fact that Christ once said: "Without Me you can do nothing." It is impossible to fight our way through the jungles of the world without His tremendous power.

Can we afford to spend our time merely watching the sins and mistakes of the people who touch our lives each day? This is really as childish as my listening to Mike swear. In a world that dazzles us with its promises, one that holds before us strange attractive guises, we need God more than ever. Can we let prayer become something for which we have no time? How we need to keep our communication with God free and strong in our day of bewilderment and change!

We must search for ways to help the Mikes of the world in prayer at the dawn of each new day. In our struggling to do good, Christ must be with us or our words and actions will take on the jangling of harsh bells that have neither feeling nor meaning.

Perhaps we have forgotten about Peter who stood in the courtyard warming his hands that momentous night when Christ was being tried. Peter, who had boasted of his loyalty, was now cut off from his Master. He had depended on his own strength and now it was gone. Maybe he had lost it in the garden when Christ had told him to pray and Peter had slept while the comforting presence of his Master was near, giving him security. Now he was alone and the questioning voice of a simple girl unnerved him and caused him to panic. The words, "You too are a Galilean, for even your speech betrays you," played hide-and-seek with his troubled memories.

Peter, relying on his own strength, is so much the little girl I was, and — to a certain extent — still am. I am so busy watching the issues at stake that I forget to pray. I must talk to God about the people who are playing a part on the same stage that I am. If my prayers are weak I will stumble over my lines, miss cues, and on the whole spoil the act. If while watching the world and lamenting its shallowness, I forget God, my role in life will be empty, regardless of how much good I seem to be doing.

The God of love is so near to us, and yet we look for some type of magic to solve our problems and those of others. Evidently we disregard the fact that He is not a disinterested God in the sky, but a God who left heaven to die for us.

5

God's Country

Sister and I drove through the hills with the rain beating against the windshield, while the wipers went back and forth in monotonous time. All week long I had looked forward to this. In the midst of turmoil I had thought: "Lord, come Friday after school I will be on my way to a blissful weekend, to a place where I can relax and just be myself."

We had reached Potter County now (God's country, as it is called). The trees were wearing skirts of misty-green. In spite of the weather I felt gay and happy. Sister sang and her song blended with the rain, then was carried away to the very tops of the hills.

Suddenly she stopped singing and said, "Hang on; we have a flat." We studied each other in dismay.

"Do you know how to change a tire?" I asked. But before she answered I knew she didn't. There was nothing to do but walk to the garage. I reached for my rain veil, and wished I had taken my umbrella instead of leaving it hanging on a hook at the convent. (I hate to carry an umbrella.)

Now a practical person would tell me that I should have thought ahead. Besides one of us should have known all about the car, but knowing too much is a dull business, making life a boring thing. Five men offered to help us, and within a short time we were on our way. It was still raining a listless rain that was neither hot nor cold. But there was a song in my heart, and I felt warm and happy inside. I had just seen human nature at its best. This land was wild and beautiful too, as if God had dropped it right into my life so that just for a little while I could dream and think without interruption.

The men who stopped to help us typified the attitude of the people in Potter County — kind, humorous, thoughtful, helpful. It seems to me that is Christianity at its best. Our bruised world does not need our factual words of wisdom. It has already had these fed to it in large doses. It craves understanding and love, not cold logic, nor theological theories. Not all the saints have held a theology book in one hand and a study of rights and freedom in the other.

If I am not mistaken we have had saints from all walks of life, from those who could neither read nor write to those great intellectual giants like St. Thomas Aquinas and St. Bonaventure. However, the silver thread that ran through their lives was one of "love." This was the essence of their spirituality, one which they never ignored.

The men who fixed the tire for us did not explain all the parts, nor did they act superior because they knew how to fix flat tires and we didn't. To explain it to me would have been a waste of time. One of the men showed us the tire, and drew our attention to the place where a sharp object had gone through it, also that it was a new tire.

He seemed worried about it. However, he didn't give us a long lecture as to how Sister should drive to avoid anything like this. Somehow I don't think a religious lecture helps either, for those we meet each day want understanding, not explanations.

Our world today has become complex, and full of problems. It is a world where we sprout a "new" spirituality, putting on an extra veneer in the form of "up-to-date" ideas on each project we undertake. We have taken our spirituality and sterilized it so that even though we speak eloquently of a "social gospel" we say nothing because our hearts are not in it. Have we lost our sense of wonder, and with it our humor? The world seems to hang on squeaking hinges that have a tendency to attempt to convince people that heaven can be won by its power alone. Its laughter is shallow and without mirth. God has become such a practical God that faith has been lost among the ruins of its broken dreams. Archbishop Robert J. Dwyer writes: ". . . We are all so dreadfully solemn. We are all so glumly convinced that upon us the ends of history have fallen. Time was when we dared to laugh a little at one another, even at ourselves. Now we talk of love all day and wallow naked in our discontents all through the night.

"But the malady is not peculiar to the Church nor confined to the Cathedral close. It is endemic in the world. The Death of God was preceded by the Death of Humor. For only one such piece of nonsense could possibly have suggested the other."

And so we have become a sober people, lost in the muddle of our own mistakes, which we neither dare acknowledge nor admit. Laughter has fled since we are so busy finding our own identity that we have forgotten to look for God. We no longer wish to live by faith. That is why we whisper to our puzzled hearts what Pilate asked the Son of God so long ago: "What is truth?" We are too busy to wait for the answer.

Time is slipping from our limp grasp and we must perform our mission in life or we will fail. But what mission? If we do not love God all is lost. Spiritually it is like having a flat tire and not knowing how to fix it, only it is far more serious. We feel our own petty worries are too much for His Majesty the King to handle. So we do not bother asking Him to blow up our dull existence with the strength of His love.

The answers are with Christ, the Son of God who let Himself be nailed to a cross and who hung for three long hours — a failure for all the world to see. During this time He never compromised and His followers never will if they are worthy of the name of Christian.

It is possible for all of us to make mistakes, to fail. Yet the biggest mistake and failure, it seems to me, is to neglect the God who left heaven to die for us. We have no right to do this, no right to forget Him, for we will never save the world unless our friendship with Him is real and lasting. It takes a long time, and much striving to fall in love with the hidden God, a long time for many of us to believe firmly that we can do all things if He strengthens us.

6

On Changing Our Plans

We began "Forty Hours" today. The chapel was heavy with heat, and I was tired, especially spiritually weary of doing good. I had planned all the things I would do this summer. It didn't turn out that way — God had other plans. Somehow, I wish I could say I didn't mind.

At the end of the first day of teaching English in a stuffy classroom, I waded through pools of self-pity, which finally turned into an unreasonable sea of anger. My mind simply burnt itself out, like the fireworks on a Fourth of July night. When the sound of the rising bell woke me from a sound sleep the next morning I was back to normal. My thoughts were quiet and subdued like dust after a heavy rainstorm.

As I made my hour before Christ in the Blessed Sacrament, I kept thinking of St. Peter. Deep within him burned a real desire to follow Christ; yet he failed again and again. Peter saw Christ one day walking on the water of the sea. It was evening and he did not recognize Him. Was it the mist, the tumbling of the waves or just that Peter was tired, seeing only a touch of gathering darkness before him?

At any rate, someone in the boat shouted, "It is the

Lord." At these words Peter became alive. Gone was the lethargy of a moment before the words had been spoken. The spray of the sea dripped unheeded from his hair as he called in thrilled excitement: "Bid me to come to You across the waters."

The God of love's voice rose and was caught in a rough breeze. "Come!" St. Peter climbed quickly over the edge of the boat, then walked over the water toward the God who controlled all nature. It occurred to Simon, as he took his eyes from the Lord who ruled the waves for just one quick second, that there were threatening waves all about him.

It flashed through his brain that men never walked on the water. How could he, Peter, do such an unnatural thing? It was at this very moment that he felt the water give way under his feet. Peter, the rugged fisherman, was terrified as he stretched his hands toward the God-Man crying out wildly, "Lord, save me. . . ."

Was there a twist of amusement on the lips of Christ as He held out His hand to His favorite Apostle saying, "Oh, you of little faith, why did you doubt?" There is much that can be read between those lines: "I am God. Why don't you trust Me? Could I ever let anything happen to you if you believed that I was capable of everything, that My strength was supreme?"

Did a strong tenderness stir the human heart of Christ when He saw this huge man covered with water, terrified at the peril the sea and his own quick doubt had brought upon him?

How often we have done the same! We have felt the light of love coming gently toward us until it is full on our face — then gone. The world quickly swallows it up in a pool of pain and misunderstanding before we have a chance to recognize its value and reality. It is then we feel a heavy, irresistible fatigue slowly sweeping over our spirit.

We have almost held hands with happiness, and now it has escaped us. Into our hearts steals an unquiet spirit as well as a sense of futility. Is it because we have turned from Christ who walks on the troubled water of our time? Are we afraid He cannot save us when we are tempted, or find that our dreams are a broken, splintered mess?

The weather has been hot this summer. Even the wind has ceased to sigh in the treetops. It seldom rains, and when it does, the rain has to be coaxed out of the clouds by thunder and lightning. The grass has turned from green to a dull brown; it lies like a faded carpet on lawns and in the meadows. It is almost human as it gives a last gasp before it turns to a dead color, while its blades seem to beg for water. Even nature cannot afford all sunlight.

It is easy to become that way spiritually — to look only for the sunshine of happiness, forgetting that we need the showers of pain and sorrow to keep us spiritually healthy and balanced.

The people in Jerusalem who stood watching on Calvary the day Christ died for the world did not bask in shimmering light, ecstasy and vision. It was dark there and the air was penetrated with pain. Those who were present had no idea that this Christ sagging on a cross between heaven and earth had a vital part in their lives.

It wasn't easy for them to look through a haze of blood at the tortured, horribly bruised Christ, then say, "This is my God." Only a handful believed in Him. Religion for them had become brown and parched. It lacked the love to make it live. But were those people any worse or better than we are? If we had been there, would we perhaps have been appalled at the awfulness of the scene? Would we have hurried from Calvary, our eyes wide with fear, trying to shed a memory which we did not want to keep?

To love Christ means to accept Him in the little everyday things of life. It means smiling when all our plans have been twisted and crippled; it is a realization of the fact that we should be willing to suffer with Him.

Are we friends of Christ? Can He ask us for anything, even for our dearest possession, and know that we will never shake our heads and run through the streets of the world looking for a chimerical savior who will not ask so much?

7

Was It Meant for Me?

A few Sisters and I had given instructions in a little town — for me they had been glorious days. As I awoke I looked up at the hills. They were lovely in the morning light with blue serene skies as a backdrop. We were leaving that day since our work was done, but I wanted to linger, to remain just a little longer. I sighed, and my morning prayer was forgotten, buried somewhere among the picturesque trees swaying in the gentle breeze.

My mind hesitated, then moved quickly to the memory of fantastic movies I have seen where a group of people are marooned on a desert island or some paradise on earth where a barrier of mountains keeps them away from the rest of the world forever. I thought how wonderful it would be if a locked gate would keep me hidden in these hills, at least for just a little longer.

It occurred to me that more serious people never enjoy these movies, usually thinking them wild and impossible. But movies like these always make me laugh since they are so absurd, so different in approach. I can always see myself in them — wanting to live peacefully instead of dangerously, wanting to be with people who love and understand me.

Regardless of how long it has been since I read and absorbed fairy tales, I still can't keep completely before my mind the idea that although fairy tales are based on life, life really is not a fairy tale. Cold fear reaches for me threateningly in the thought that obedience may someday lock me out of this town and send me to a place without warmth, where I would feel unwanted. Courage is not one of my strong points. Some of my readers have perhaps read between the lines or beyond them and detected the lack of this trait. I like peace and quiet, and I thrive when they are present. But when darkness falls and the stars drop out of the sky one by one, I don't want to be around. Let someone else light the candles and fight the battles; I will retreat into the stillness of the hills and be at rest.

In reading the Gospels I wonder how Christ felt when He visited Mary and Martha at Bethany. Did He wish to remain for just a little longer? There were no Pharisees there to tangle up His words and ask Him to give an account of every unguarded phrase, every statement. Somehow I wonder if the human Christ didn't want to stay just a little longer. He could have done so many things which would have been an easy way out. But Christ didn't. He just kept on going when He knew that someday the end would come, and somewhere He would be crucified on a lonely hill by the very ones He had tried to help — those He had so desperately wanted to save. How courageous He was, how realistic!

Brave words come naturally when we are not faced with danger. But to make the words come alive we must act, even though what we do leads us on a lonely road where sniper fire strikes us. As we travel that road we should be careful not to become slaves to the opinion of those around us in order to avoid the discomfort of being shot at from ambush. A true follower of the God-Man must close his heart and mind to the idea of putting "safety" first in his life. If we place human esteem before what we think is right, we sell Christ, not for thirty pieces of silver, but for a messy pottage of face-saving. Our hearts become old, fearful of every voice and movement that will cause others to think less of us. Peace at all costs is not really peace, but only a camouflage for hypocrisy and cowardice. Christ expects us to be true to Him and to ourselves. We cannot do this if we are swayed with every wind of opinion that blows hot or cold around us.

There is no such thing even in our age of quick and easy ways of doing things, as a "push-button" spirituality which we can use when all other means have failed. We still must seek the answers in prayer or we will live a pretense without even mediocre spirituality. We will be bored with what everyone thinks is right, and with causes in which we have never really believed. It is necessary to keep and hold to our hearts the warmth and love of the living God who came to earth and died a horrible death for us. In so doing He made it possible for us to dream and think and believe as His followers, knowing that we could be wrong; knowing, too, that we do not have all the answers. Yet in the turmoil of our days we must have deep faith that the Holy Spirit will be with us, guiding us regardless of how rough the road may be. This to me is peace and love. It is the path the Son of God would want us to follow.

As Thomas Merton has written: ". . . Therefore will I trust You always though I seem to be lost and in the shadow of death. I will not fear, for You are ever with me, and You will never leave me to face my perils alone."

8

Promises to Keep

It was a hot stuffy day when I came upon my mother and Mrs. Dragone talking in the kitchen. I was on my way to the clothesline to hang up my bathing suit when something Mrs. Dragone was saying in a small sad voice caught my attention. "I haven't seen Helen, Lucille and Bernice for years. But you know I can't just leave Mother and go to California. If someone would stay with her at night. But I can't get anyone; no one wants to do it. I — "

By now I had become interested and I interrupted, saying, "I'll stay with her."

Both my mother and Mrs. Dragone turned and looked at me. Mrs. Dragone finally said: "Honey, you'd have to stay with her every night and she locks the door at eight. Sometimes she's hard to manage."

"I know," I said, but I really didn't know.

Since there wasn't anymore I could say, I picked up my bathing suit from the back of the chair and started for the door. I heard Mrs. Dragone ask, with hope creeping into her voice: "Do you think she could?"

I closed the screen door quietly and heard Mother say, "Yes, if she told you she would, she will."

So Mrs. Dragone went off to California to visit with

her daughters for six weeks. Now, when I promised to stay with Mrs. Paukette — who at ninety was as wrinkled and brown as an ancient oak, and as set in her ways — I had no idea what it would entail.

I just felt very noble, but before long that feeling was gone. The nights were hot and stifling. Mrs. Paukette didn't like air. I did, but it was her house, so I just looked at the storm window, wishing with all my heart that the whole thing would fall out. But I knew it never would. Sometimes when I couldn't sleep I thought of my room at home with its open window.

There I could see the maple trees and hear the wind sighing softly through the leaves. And I could always see the stars. At times like these I would try to convince myself that Mrs. Dragone wouldn't be gone long, but six weeks was as long as six years for a fourteen-year-old girl who loved her freedom.

One evening I was having such a good time I forgot about Mrs. Paukette. When I finally realized what time it was, I was conscience-stricken. June and Allan were with me. When Allan saw how worried I was, he tried to convince me that I should go home. After all, Mrs. Paukette would be all right for just one night. "No, Allan," I argued, "I promised I would stay every night. By now she has the door locked. And she won't hear me rap; she's stone-deaf."

"I'll make her hear," Allan assured me.

"Only if you break down the door!"

When we arrived Allan began to pound on the door. I looked at him in alarm. Was he really trying to break it down?

Finally there were footsteps, and I heard the bolt being drawn back. The door opened and there stood Mrs. Paukette leaning heavily on her cane and peering up at me. "What made you so late?" she inquired point-blank.

I turned to thank June and Allan, but they were already on their youthful, free way. The remainder of that night was much the same as other confining nights I had spent with Mrs. Paukette.

By the time the six weeks were almost gone I began to watch daily for a possible earlier return of Mrs. Dragone. I used to stand on the rusty bridge and wait for the bus. Sometimes I would lean my arms on the railing and look at the water below. It was running indifferently over smooth rocks. The summer was dry, and even the brook seemed tired of waiting for rain. When the bus came and went, and Mrs. Dragone didn't appear, I would go home and say dejectedly to Mother, "Mrs. Dragone wasn't on the bus."

She would look at me and say quietly, "Maybe she'll come tomorrow. Sit down and eat your supper." My father and brothers with warm understanding said nothing. Although they were always sympathetic, they never pitied me.

Years later I knelt before an altar and made a vow: "I promise poverty, chastity, obedience, conversion of morals, and stability according to the rule of St. Benedict."

The chapel was filled with the scent of roses and God was very near. Life spread out before me like a magic carpet: blue skies would be above me — the soft music of spiritual success would be all around me. Yes, "Nuns dream sometimes," especially young nuns.

When Sisters who had experienced spiritual battles hinted that someday the stars could go out of my sky, I laughed and said, "Yes, I know." But I really didn't know. I just felt young and full of joy. After all, I could still reach up and touch the stars. Youth does not know that what bounces up so thrillingly is apt to come back down with a jarring bump.

Poverty? What did it mean to me? I had known people poor in material things, yet exceedingly happy. That wouldn't be too hard to take. But I didn't know that the God I had vowed to serve also required a poverty of spirit, one that would be satisfied with His love alone. The God of Calvary asked that I give my love without asking to be repaid by the people I served. Neither did I know the meaning of complete poverty; I must surrender *me*. From here on it would have to be, "Not my will, but Thine be done." That would never be easy for anyone who is human.

Chastity was not a negative thing either. In a world that glorified sex I would have to develop a deep, real love of the crucified God so I could love His world just a tiny bit as much as He did on the cross, paying the price and never asking a return. If sex could be glorified in loose physicality, why could it not be more glorious in chaste spirituality?

Sometimes, however, spirituality runs indifferently, just as the little brook when I waited for Mrs. Dragone. The end when I would see God face-to-face could be very far. There would be days when tears of loneliness burned behind my eyes, and everything would seem hopeless, but I had to go on because I told Him that I would.

Obedience in our world today, where we excuse ourselves with the easy words, "We are only human," is made to appear unreasonable. Yet in the chapel I had one day promised God that I would obey.

I had really said: "I'll go where You want me to go, do what you want me to do." I was not out of my mind then, neither am I now, and I am still "only human." But I didn't know how difficult that promise would be to keep, or that I would have to fight myself every step of the way.

Conversion of morals was like saying to God, "I'll keep on trying. I may fall again and again, but I'll pull myself up and go on. I'll try to let the failures in life make me bigger and I know they'll make me more humble, and more tolerant and understanding of weakness in others."

Then comes the last vow which is so important in the latter part of our twentieth century since many religious are leaving the convent for various reasons. Stability, I think, says: "I won't ever run away from You, God, no matter how hard life becomes. Help me to see the light of Your love when night descends upon me and I no longer know the way."

If I had gone home the night I was locked out by Mrs. Paukette, if I had tried the door of my own home, it would have been opened. My mother would have looked surprised; my father would have perhaps said quietly, "You should have watched the time." My brothers would have raised their eyebrows. That would have been all. Yet, they would have been disappointed in me.

In the religious life, as in any other life, there are times when we feel everything is useless, and we are tempted to walk away. At times like these we must stand on the rusty bridges of the world and wait. When we are weary of fighting a meaningless battle, the God of hosts is still with us. He is watching; He will stretch out His hand to guide us when all the lights in our world have gone out, and there is not even the flicker of one small candle in the darkness around us.

9

Shadowland

Last night I could not sleep, so I got out of bed and sat in a chair by the window looking into the night. The lights from the school cast long shadows on the lilac bush beneath my window. Sounds came drifting in through the open window — the endless chirp of crickets, the croaking of frogs, the angry barking of a dog in the distance, the rumbling of traffic. By and by I thought of the surgery I had undergone a little more than two weeks ago.

The evening before surgery the doctor made a routine, momentary visit. There was only one thing in that brief conversation I could remember. That was his asking me if I were nervous.

Now I do not pretend to have the heroism of a martyr. I may accept aches and pains with a minimum of complaints. Yet I am delighted when God removes them, nor do I ever ask that He give me pain, even when I am on the highest peak of spiritual aspiration. But I experienced some sort of vague comfort in having met the surgeon, a tall pleasant, friendly man. There was something about him which dispelled my fear, leaving me with a sense of confidence and a feeling of trust. It wasn't what he said, but rather his tone of voice, quiet with a personal touch.

When I replied "No," the doctor looked at me strangely. Perhaps I imagined it, but I thought he raised polite eyebrows, while a flicker of doubt wavered in his eyes. Then he was gone.

For some time after the operation I lay as still as possible since every movement hurt. My whole body was a maddening mixture of pain and weariness. I wished desperately to be able to toss all this aside, to get out of bed, to leave the hospital and be well again. A footstep caused me to turn my head. Profiled against the still, shiny light stood the doctor. My mind fumbled for words, and they came tumbling out unadorned. "Doctor, yesterday I almost had the nurses take me down to the operating room, and have you put back everything you took out."

Immediately he was beside me with words that were gentle and soothing. "Now, Sister, you don't want anything we took out of you put back."

Understanding ran like a murmur through my mind and I must have fallen asleep since I felt an irresistible tiredness.

Perhaps you wonder why I am telling you all this when it doesn't mean anything except to me. As I sat at my window last night, my hospital experience and the vast difference between duty and confidence in God filled my mind. Duty is a straitjacket word which conveys to the mind strange images. But confidence is a personal thing that leaves a feeling of the power and strength of another.

God never warms our hearts unless we have confidence in Him. Oh, we may be careful not to disobey Him, but that is our duty. It keeps us in the small realm of an impersonal love. We have become duty-bound Christians who never really trust God with our hopes, and dreams, and failures. We do not let Him into the domain of our anguish and fear. Our prayers and lives are mechanical with no intimately personal feeling for this God who lived among a people whose materialism was as great as ours.

He knew that they neither trusted nor loved Him; that someday they would crucify Him on a bleak hillside. In the chaos of those tremendous moments, with voices nimble in mimicry ringing in their ears, some of the people who had been at one time impressed with the goodness of Christ ran from Calvary. With confidence destroyed, they went on living their sickly lives.

The people of our day give Christ the coin of the temple, then forget Him. Their vision is blurred. They have forgotten that as the divine Physician He has the answer to all spiritual ills. I do think one of the problems of our twentieth century is a lack of confidence in the strength of Christ, tending to impersonalize Him to such an extent that relationship with Him becomes "weary, stale, flat and unprofitable."

Spiritual pain comes to all of us in varying ways. We may feel superficially noble someday and tell God He may have His way with us. Then, when He has cut into our lives, and removed something which did not belong there in the first place, we grow fearful and call out in fright, "I want it back." If we were to listen, we would hear Christ's voice in our hearts whispering reassuring words.

We overlook the healing competence of Christ as we plow ruthlessly through the fields and meadows of earth looking for the alchemist's cure-all. We are unconscious of anything but duty fulfilled. So our spiritual life rots and ceases to be a joy. We become spiritual sadists, losing sight of happiness and becoming creatures of duty. And God waits with divine patience for us to come to Him in trust.

10

They Were an Inspiration

The campus at St. Bonaventure University is beautiful, with a charm that is all its own. Yet this isn't what I want to tell you about today, not the quiet comfort of the hills, nor the peace that prevails, but about a group of people — the cafeteria staff. Never have I seen a kinder, more considerate and understanding group of people than these.

They are always ready to put themselves out to accommodate anyone. When I went through the line, I always liked to watch them, solicitous of the needs of each individual. To these people, it seemed to me, serving food was not just a job to be done with as little exertion as possible.

They were alert to the needs of others. Putting food on plates can become a monotonous thing. I would think that the same priests, Brothers, Sisters and students who show up for meals each day would tend to become merely boring faces, seeking only to satisfy an immediate personal need and totally oblivious of the human element that provided it. Yet the ladies never seemed weary. In fact they seemed to be enjoying their job. To me they were an inspiration. Although they were strangers I feel I know them very well and that there is a common bond between us.

If we are really Christians in the true sense of the word, we should be this way in any walk of life, in any profession or occupation. We should not be uninterested beings who merely do our jobs thoroughly.

But you and I become weary of "well-doing," and forget all about the cheerful smile which needs to be given to someone who is weary and depressed. We build our own small world and furnish it with selfish aims and ambitions.

We adopt a secular code, not a way of life, in order to gain what we call our "fulfillment." But is this really living? Is it what Christ wants of us? A robot is efficient. It gets things done, but it has no heart. If we are interested only in getting work finished, if we have forgotten the needs of those who drift through our life, we cease to be Christians.

Love should be the most tremendous thing in the world for us. It should light up the dark places in our minds, making us warm when the driving winds of doubt strive to take possession of our hearts. Even when dark doubts assail us and the world is filled with puzzling confusion, we should not let the magic around us grow mercenary and tarnished. It should still be there when the sharp winds of winter leave our spirits shivering. Days when we are tired of well-doing come to all of us. I feel sure they descend upon the cafeteria staff, too. Yet, I never noticed any sign of ill temper in any of them.

In our times love is perhaps one of the most misunderstood words. We say that we love certain types of music, food and clothing. We can say we love almost anything. We see love cloaked with selfishness, a cloak which may deceive even the best of men. But love as I saw it in the cafeteria at St. Bonaventure University is genuine since it speaks with actions.

Christ paid for our souls with His blood. Calvary was dark and lonely. Because He was God as well as man, Christ saw us there cringing because we are afraid to love in the true sense of the word. He saw and felt and knew the word love would be twisted. He saw love carved into such small dimensions that it became a crippled thing. This was not the love He wished to be given to all men, regardless of race or creed.

And yet love is all about us. We see it in the white purity of sparkling winter snows; we hear it in the song of a bird; we feel it in prayer when the whole world is hushed, and only God seems to be listening. It is at our fingertips, waiting for us. We could ask God in the simplest prayers to give it to us.

Would it be possible for us to pray an unadorned prayer like this? "Give me Your love and the grace to love You night and day. When the winds blow and I am frightened, may I love You! When the sun is blazing with a heat that scorches and dries up my spirit, may I love You! When the battles of life leave me bruised and wounded, may I love You! Please, Lord, may I love You always no matter what the days may bring, or how dark the nights may be! Your love must be the most important thing that life can give. And give me the grace to spread that love wherever I may go."

11

When We Need Him

Perhaps one of the most wonderful gifts God can bestow upon us is a friend. A definition which describes this better, I think, than anything else is: "A friend is one who knows you, knows all about you, and likes you anyway."

One of my best friends is a Benedictine priest. I met him when I was teaching in a parish where he was an assistant. I won't say we always agreed on everything — we didn't. I was quick to anger, inclined to want my own way, while he was calm, apparently never letting anything ruffle him. Oh, we never had any serious arguments, but I never dreamed in those days that he would be someone I would turn to each time an event seemed to shake my world, leaving me confused.

After I was transferred, I saw him occasionally. It seemed strange, but each time something came along that worried me, he showed up like the genie when the lamp was rubbed. He always seemed to have the answer, and I could tell him exactly how I felt without shocking him or letting myself in for a long moralizing sermon.

For months now I had wanted to talk to someone who would understand. But there was no one I really felt could help. My friend was in Brazil and neither of us cared to spend time on letters which stood a very good chance of being tossed into the Amazon River. Time was too precious to both of us to run such a risk.

Spiritual people who climb mountains of sanctity might consider this a form of weakness, others might say it is nonsense, since I should be mature — the overworked word of our times — enough to solve any problem. Evidently God thinks otherwise.

It wasn't exactly a surprise when Father came, and yet it was, although I knew he had returned to the States. We talked for less than an hour, but during that time I felt the tired spiritual discouragement which had been haunting me leave. I seemed to emerge from a dark cellar where I had been locked for a long time. My friend never scolded, never brought up any failures, never preached. Once in the course of the conversation, when he sensed the laissez-faire attitude I was adopting, his tone sharpened with alarm as he said, "Sister, don't do that!"

I felt like a child trapped in the act of trying to fling away a prized possession of her parents because she did not know its value. He made me realize, without seeming to do so purposely, that I had bargained for this on the day I promised God I would love Him forever. There was no pretense between us; there never has been. I didn't try to be witty or bright. I could just be myself, knowing that even though this wasn't exactly a sparkling conversation, it would be understood. I had been standing on the edge of pools of discouragement bordering on despair, and I needed a hand to pull me back.

Real concern for our anxiety is seldom shown in our sophisticated day. Those we converse with each day are too confused to listen to the heartbreak of the sick society about them. Their world is restless, as if a giant hand has shaken all peace from its cities and towns. It aches with loneliness. Yet its people still have a scintillating charm in their voices which leads us to believe they are happy, that all is well.

It is not difficult to sense the hard metallic ring in the current coin of conversation. For many it is almost dangerous to let their thoughts catch up with their words. Often when we talk to people, we become painfully aware that they aren't listening, that they are not even vaguely interested. We want to say, "I'm sorry. I've bored you." Then slip away. Or we come away thinking, "I shouldn't have said that. They won't understand."

Many thoughts ran through my mind after I talked to my Benedictine friend. There had been a wide wound spreading through me like a river over which I had no control, a wound that needed to be stanched. What brought him to me at this critical time? Was it telepathy? Was it God? I do not believe in the former.

The human Christ in the garden of Gethsemane must have felt that all the powers of evil were alive and pressing down upon Him as He gazed into what appeared to be an empty heaven. Was there no one to understand, no one to share that awful feeling of helplessness from the beginning of time until the end? The Apostles slept on. His prayer, "If it be possible remove this chalice from Me," rocked heaven. Even the God-Man was not above crying for comfort and help.

That God in the garden made us to His image and likeness. When we cry out, when the whole world has become a tangled jungle of confused ideas, and there is no "clearing," He may not send an angel to comfort us, but He often sends a human being who takes the place of an angel.

One thing of which we may be certain in times of howling gale and driving rain, Christ is still with us. The confusion all about us makes it necessary for us to pray for calm courage and confidence. Our world will never take on the horrors of a Gethsemane, yet we have a God who went through all this pain waiting for us to ask Him for help.

We must refuse to let outside pressures invade the citadel of our souls where God must reign supreme. When the stars go out in the sky, and the lamps of heaven seem to have run out of oil, since we cannot see them burning at all, let us turn to the God who knew real darkness in a garden, and whisper in hopeful prayer, "Our Father, if it be possible remove this chalice from us."

12

Raindrops at Loretto

The alarm clock awoke me with a start at 5:30 a.m. It was raining, and I could hear a million splashes against the windowpane. I shut off the alarm and looked out. There were lights in some of the windows in the opposite wing, while on the right the woods appeared wet and depressing. Except for the sound of the rain there was a heavy stillness around me. Going to chapel at St. Francis College meant a lovely walk in nice weather. But in the rain?

By the time I stepped into the rain it had settled into a soft drizzle. The pink and red and yellow roses beside the building were beautiful even with the drops of water falling from their petals. Everything was quiet, and I felt as if I were standing alone on the edge of nowhere, surrounded by pine trees. Little streams of water ran gleefully over the pavement. I found myself walking through a puddle which splashed over my shoes and brought me back quickly to the land of reality.

When I reached the monastery chapel the Franciscans were praying their office in Latin. It made me think of my own convent. Was it only four years ago that we had prayed in Latin, or was it longer? Everything was so different then. Suddenly I was filled with nostalgia for a time and place that no longer seemed to shine upon my life.

Here I was in a strange place, praying my office in English, not Latin, and alone. I must straighten my shoulders and "get with it." But I didn't care to follow a world that no longer seemed to know or care about anything except doing what everyone else did in the same way. Nor was I unhappy in the thought. This was my life and I must live it, not by playing "follow the leader" through a luxurious culture of spring woods, but rather struggling to do the will of God in the monotonous rain and sleet of everyday annoyances.

It seemed that I could, kneeling there with the Latin chant of God's praises drifting over me, reach back and touch childhood days when I had run barefoot through puddles of water in the pouring rain. I had made mud pies almost before the last drops had fallen on the saturated earth.

And now? "But I am an adult," the small practical part of me seemed to nag angrily. "A mature person does not even remember the days when she ran through the rain as a child, and she has tossed aside the joy of making footprints on the muddy earth with her bare feet!"

Are our lives perhaps too adult, attempting to be too mature? Are we becoming old men and women who are so wrapped up in meaningless formalities that the laughter and joy of being a child are gone forever? Are we so engrossed in artificial pleasure that the beauty of God's world is lost to us?

God has asked us to love Him and we can do this only by searching for Him, even when He doesn't seem to be aware that our hearts are becoming dry and empty. But you and I are such strange people. We want to push a "prayer button" and find the answer. We want a real good, holy feeling to sweep us off our feet. So we let ourselves become tied in a spiritual knot; we long to be the kind of people God never intended us to be.

In our day we no longer look through the rain and see the pine trees of joy, the beauty of flowers. Like the emperor in Hans Christian Andersen's story "The Nightingale," we are fascinated by the musical notes of a glittering, artificial bird. Have we lost the imaginative wand of magic which changes so much dross into the gold of life?

It is still necessary to be original and real and brave enough to toss aside the commonplace so that we can look deeper into the true meaning of life. At the same time we must retain a sufficient sense of humor to be amused with the generation that proclaims, "It is stupid to conform to others. It is brilliant for others to conform to us."

There is so much confusion. Yet, God is only a prayer away. He is waiting for us to look through the raindrops glistening with bewilderment. The King is still there, even if we do not see Him clearly in the rain. We must say over and over, "My God, I love and trust You." That is not merely a psychiatric trick — it is the only way our hearts can ever find peace.

III

Autumn

*How bravely autumn paints
upon the sky
The gorgeous flame of
summer which is fled!*

— *Thomas Hood*

1

And This Is Autumn

This fall I have been assigned to a country mission hidden among the hills. The nights are quiet, since the croaking of the frogs has been silenced by the first frost which descended upon us a few weeks ago. It left behind it the magic of days filled with loveliness. Each day I walk beside the church to take my spiritual reading. Then I look over a range of ageless hills, which seem to whisper to me through their beauty that in a short time their color will be gone, and only the setting sun will light up their drabness.

There is something about autumn which I love. It carries with its splendor a gentle reminder that all things pass away; yet all of spring and summer are combined in its haunting charm.

In the autumn of our lives there are times when we become anxious, while our spirituality sags wearily. We look back over our days only to find everything we have done is tinged with the weeds of failure. The golden wheat waving in the sun appears to be nothing but a mirage in the overworked imagination of those middle years. We are older now in many ways. The blazing sunshine of summer with its heavy heat is not unknown to us. There have been wild storms during summer nights with crashing thunder and frightening lightning. But our buoyancy kept us going, kept us young at heart. Oh, it wasn't that we were without fear, but spiritually we didn't become so weary of well-doing. The road seemed smoother in those far-away days, and we didn't feel like sitting down beside a stream or escaping into a quiet wood, since the magic of spring and summer kept our spirits high.

Then came a spiritual autumn with all its changes to challenge us when we were tired of fighting. We felt the sharp thrust of autumn frosts reach out and chill our hearts. The road became rocky and rough while we became fearful.

In this world of ours that changes with the rapidity of the leaves in autumn we want to run away into the quiet forests of spiritual bliss. We wish with all our hearts to feel once more the cool, gentle breezes of God's love all about us, and to watch the stars at night glitter comfortingly through softly stirring leaves.

But this is not the worst. A spiritual inertia descends upon us. It laughs at our dreams, distorts everything out of its true proportion, making us think we were not made for greater things. Yet, if we think of the seasons, isn't this autumn to be expected after the spring rains and summer storms? And isn't God's glory in the red and yellow and orange leaves that cover the ground with their silent beauty as meaningful? By this time our spirituality should have become mature.

The autumn of our life should be a time of harvesting, of taking our thoughts and our dreams and sorting them. It should mean the reexamining of our motives, and tossing away the habits of the past that are covered with mildew. But most of all it is a time for appreciating the life of Christ as an inexhaustible exemplar for every phase of human life.

From a very human point of view Christ accomplished little. Oh, He had cured the sick and made the lame walk, but what was that? The Roman soldiers at His crucifixion probably yawned with boredom as His life drew to a close. There was nothing left to do; they had already thrown dice for His clothes. Christ had gambled, and, it seemed, had tossed away His love. The stars of Bethlehem were gone, the hills of Nazareth were a faraway dream. And yet Christ refused to come down from the cross, refused to compromise because He loved.

Appreciation, like the harvest, comes only with autumn. It is not a gift. It needs to grow.

2

A Steeplejack

The mission convent was so close to the church that from the window I could look up at the steeple where the men were repairing the roof and cross. If you were an alarmist and watched them, you feared for them. Were they sure, when they were up so high, that everything was in order?

One day, as I paused in the basement (which was also used for the boys' sacristy) to put my cleaning material away, the door opened. I saw one of the steeplejacks face-to-face. As he dropped his ropes and other equipment, he smiled. We struck up a conversation. He told me much about his life in that short talk. I do not remember his name; in fact, I do not recall his telling me what it was. But since I never expected to see him again, it didn't matter much. He was a steeplejack, I was a nun, and we let it go at that.

One of the first things I asked him was if he ever became frightened when he looked down from such a great height. His reply was that he had faith in the hooks, ropes, harnesses, and all the other equipment he used. "In this business," he said, "there are very few people — that is why the pay is very good. Besides, it gives you a chance to see the country."

He wanted to talk, and I was an interested listener. He told me that he had become a steeplejack when he was quite young. He had traveled through much of the country — twenty-four states to be exact — repairing churches. Then a smile flickered across his face, and loneliness tiptoed through his eyes as he said with a note of sadness creeping into his voice, "Although I am forty I have never married. On this job it is not good to worry about a wife and children."

I never saw him again. Sometimes when I kneel before Christ in the tabernacle I ask Him to be near the man with the weather-beaten face who repaired so many of His churches and did not seem to know the meaning of fear. Often I wonder, too, if this steeplejack ever lost his nerve.

As Christians we should climb heights. But it is easy to lose our nerve. You and I need a shot of steeplejack blood in our veins. Perhaps then we would not lose our nerve so easily. True, the steeplejack could see results; we seldom do. That is one of the reasons why it is so difficult to keep the flame of courage burning in our hearts.

We long for the height, but fear the depth within us. We have forgotten in our time of fear that God is for the fearful. Once we heard the now-forgotten words David uttered long ago: "Though I should walk in the shadow of death I will fear no evil, for Thou art with me." God is with us too in these troubled times when security implies restlessness. He is with us when we are puzzled by everything that is happening to our world.

We become modern Humpty Dumpties who feel our wall of understanding crumbling beneath us, and all the king's horses and all the king's men will never be able to put our confused lives together again. We lose our nerve, even when we are trying to save ourselves.

Why are we so fearful? We have infinitely better

equipment than the steeplejack. Christ's love is the unbreakable rope that holds us securely. The sacraments are the hooks attached to His lifeline. But rope and hooks are of no value unless we have nerve enough to use them.

Calvary was far above the heights my steeplejack ever dared to ascend. Steeplejacks are brave men; yet One who was meek and humble did not hesitate. Although He was both God and man, He had to rely on man's nerve to make the climb. And the man in Him had the nerve to stay there in spite of all the forces within and without that would have made Him come down.

Even in His pain His bloodshot eyes saw through those who stood about the cross. Many of them were present when He said, "If any man will come after Me, let him deny himself, and take up his cross daily, and follow Me." But many of them did not have the nerve. Cold chills caressed their minds, paralyzing them. Fear drove them from Him.

My casual steeplejack friend did not ask me to try his rope and hooks. However, from the greater height of Calvary came a challenge, "Follow Me." Do I have the nerve? If I am to follow Christ, my love cannot be merely reasonable. It must have a streak of madness in it.

3

I Just Couldn't Say Good-bye

There is a wistful sadness about September. Summer has sighed at the idea of relinquishing its sparkling days and warm green meadows and woods. It has left its signature, "Regretfully yours," on the maple leaves which still carry patches of pale green on their vivid scarlet. The song of birds has ceased, while a chill has crept stealthily into the early morning air.

There is a day which tiptoes tauntingly through my memory begging for an audience, the day in early September when I said good-bye to the world I loved. I walked to town in the afternoon with my hands thrust deep in my raincoat pockets. There was a lovely misty rain falling softly on the pavement. It didn't matter, even though I had always loved to walk in the rain. My heart was heavy and sick. My feelings were those Cinderella must have felt in the fairy tale I used to know by heart.

Someone had asked me to mail a letter; after that I was going to a show. I didn't want to think. When I came out of the post office I saw Larry coming toward me. I didn't want to see anyone I knew either. My mind was weary. I had struggled with arguments for months, examined them, put them aside, then started all over again. It was better to slip away, not to say good-bye, not to tell any of my friends I was doing anything so absurd as entering a convent. If only I could disappear at this moment or hide somewhere, but it was too late — Larry had seen me. I had always enjoyed talking to him, but not now.

Larry was in no hurry. He talked on and on. The rain had stopped; the sun came out from behind a cloud, sending dazzling colors through the wet leaves. Tears burned behind my eyes, fighting to be free. I evaded questions about what I was going to do, hiding behind words as if I were carrying on a guerrilla warfare.

At last he was gone and I was once more alone with my thoughts. This was reality — a parting with people I knew and loved. It was like kissing a dream good-bye. Something was slipping from my life, and inside of me there was a wild panic which did not correspond with the lazy soft-shoe of my feet on the damp concrete.

The break from my comfortable world of friends and sights was clean; I never saw most of them again; yet I never quite forgot them. They belonged to the meadows of springtime blooming with poppies and buttercups, a time when I was young and carefree. And somehow, I wanted to always keep them in my prayers. Sometimes it is like playing a game of solitaire in my mind — putting the cards on the table, wondering how life has worked out for these friends from the world I left behind.

Their lives are always shrouded in mystery. Some nuns, and those outside the convent, too, might think this is most impractical, but then I am not a practical person. Looking at the world with its never-ceasing search for peace of soul, I feel sad that it cannot help itself, and I have no desire to copy its practicality.

It is not always easy to follow God's plans for us, to make our hearts believe that He will remove all the mold and despair that clutter up our souls if we simply trust His love and strength. There are times when our hearts feel a sudden emptiness and a shocking sense of loss, days when we are puzzled and bewildered at all the changes going on around us. We really do not know what to do about it all. We look into the future which seems to force us to exchange our freedom for a neurotic secondhand sort of spirituality, and we are frightened — terribly afraid. What has happened to all the warmth in religion which made us feel so secure? Life's storms take on gigantic proportions, and the God of love we were so sure of seems to have left our lifeboat when we needed Him most.

During times when God has put us on a spiritual diet it is easy simply to drift, to be neither very bad nor very good. We agree with people because it is the simplest thing to do. We are afraid of becoming different. No one must think of us as anything but the usual average character to whom he is always talking and listening. Finally we acquire a sameness that makes our cardboard spirituality collapse into a shapeless heap.

If only we would let Christ invade our hearts instead of wrapping them up in a cocoon of public opinion! Our life would take on a glow, and He would shine forth in us just as the sun shone on the leaves the September day I told you about, removing all the damp sogginess. But fear takes us by the hand, and instead of shining forth in us, Christ has to make way for this invader. Christ waits for us to cease existing and really live. We are trapped in the meshes of a world which makes wild, desperate noises as it struggles to claim us. The sound of its knuckles upon our hearts threatens us, making God seem more remote than ever.

Our days of materialism and incessant change make chameleons of us all. If we do not counsel with "the way, the truth and the life" we become dull, insipid individuals who are always afraid of what the crowd might think. We lead our mediocre lives in the marketplaces of the world. Our smiles are fixed and without warmth, since we do not wish to smile at the wrong times, in the wrong places.

A life that neglects the God who told us that without Him we can do nothing is as strange and distorted as that of Dismas until his eyes were opened and he recognized the God so close to him.

4

A Memory

Sometimes there are wisps of memories that slide across my mind and beg to be recognized and dreamed about after a long, long time has elapsed. My reminiscences of Jane are like that. They came to me one day when the sun wasn't shining so brightly, and my world was in a fog of modern ideas which seemed cold and barren.

Jane was the best friend I ever had before I entered the convent. She was gay, lovely and popular. Yet there was a seriousness about her which was hard to fathom, for underneath there seemed to be a beautiful spirituality which I do not think anyone but God really saw.

When I entered the convent Jane was disturbed; she didn't think it was the wisest thing I had ever done. In spite of this, she wrote to me for a number of years. She told me about her uncle offering to pay her way through college — then in the next sentence explained that she had no desire to be a teacher as he wanted her to be, and had refused to accept his offer.

Once I received a letter from Jane telling me she had broken her leg while skiing. In one of the letters that followed she wrote that her uncle had finally decided to let her take a two-year business course as she had wanted to do for a long time. Letters to me grew fewer and fewer then, until the last and final letter.

Since Jane was not an emotional person, the letter was direct and frank; it read:

"I would not tell this to anyone but you since you know how much I thought of Jim. He came home from the seminary a few months ago and asked me for a date. I went out with him, and it seemed like old times, except that the gang wasn't there. During his last vacation he asked me to go out again, and became very insistent. He called me at the office and at home but I refused to go. I don't think I will ever love anyone but Jim, but if he has a vocation to the priesthood, I don't want to be the one to come between God and him. . . ."

I do not remember the rest of the letter. The curtain had dropped between Jane and me, for I never again heard from her, nor of her, nor did I ever see her again. I did learn about Jim, though, from someone who knew him. He went on and became a devoted priest.

And now today it seems that I am sitting in a dark auditorium waiting for the curtain to rise on the second act and reveal to me how things worked out for my friend Jane.

If only we had the courage that Jane did, we would never let anything come between our love and God, but we do. Christ is our life — whoever loves Him will be at peace with himself. Yet we forget this while the world takes on a swollen, dulled confusion as we are swept into its tangled noise.

Christ hanging in the sky in lonely pain that first Good Friday saw us just as we are today. There were people there whose culture was different, but who were very much like us in their thinking. Even the high priests and the leaders of the people had condemned Christ. The ordinary people watched each other with trepidation, with suspicion and with fear. Dared they become known as a follower of One whom their supposed intellectual superiors condemned as a charlatan?

This was the beginning of a new epic, a strange unknown age, that was not sure, that felt uncertainty quicken in their veins as they watched the life fade out of Christ. And as the wind blew over the bloody face of this man who claimed to be the Son of God and the darkness grew denser, they turned from Calvary and fled.

We are so quick to condemn them, to think, "Had we been there upon that hill we would have been different." But would we? Their leaders had condemned Him; there was no glory in Him. The only thing they saw was the blood flowing from His hands and feet, His twisted, tortured face. They only heard the murmuring of the crowd, the words of hate tossed at Him. Between their love and the God on the cross slid distrust in its commonest form. They were afraid of what would happen to them if they threw in their lot with this man whose very love had seemed to be the cause of His crucifixion.

We have become a fearful people. We hear the noise of contradiction all about us, and we let it come between the God of love and us. We hear it said by even the best men: "Surely all of those good people cannot be wrong." So we go along and let those about us form our conscience by telling us what we should do, what we should say, and even whom we should love.

And we no longer dream, for dreams are such impractical things and we are realists. And yet, if we cease to dream and hope and love, what have we but an empty world that has come between God and us? It becomes a world whose laughter is no longer heard, since most people have taken themselves much too seriously.

Life is short, and especially in this space-age of wars and riots and unrest, we must remember to beg Him to hold our failing faith in nail-pierced hands so that we never cease to laugh and love and hope that nothing comes between Him and us.

5

Yesterday and Today

Somewhere in my desk, buried among plays, articles and other writings I have done, is a pageant which another Sister and I wrote when our community celebrated its centennial. Every once in a while I take it from the drawer and leaf through it. It has such fascinating memories — memories that are good and wholesome and alive.

The Sister who wrote the pageant with me was quite different from me. We didn't even agree on the characters. My sympathies were with Mother Benedicta, the foundress of our community; hers were with Abbot Wimmer, then Benedictine superior of the district, whom I considered austere and cold. But the strange part about the whole thing was that we never quarreled. She was older than I, with much more experience in the religious life, and also very tactful. The important thing was that she respected my views and was willing to listen. It seemed that I was always asking her, "Why?" She never refused to explain.

During the time I wrote and directed the pageant I learned more about the community than I ever had before or have since. It was a merging of the past and the present. How different their culture had been; how bound up with the customs of their native Germany! The hard lives of the nuns and the sacrifices they made thrilled me. How heroic they were! And yet, in our materialistic day we would prejudge them as foolhardy, impractical women fighting for a lost cause.

There were problems then, even as there are now. Humanly speaking, these Benedictines who lived a century ago often faced insurmountable obstacles. Sometimes their views were intolerably narrow, but that was typical of their day. A sample of this was their refusal to accept other nationalities into the community.

"I can't see it," I would say over and over. "Why were they so straitlaced?"

And Sister would reply with infinite patience, "You have to remember in writing this that theirs was a different age, a different era, a different culture."

In spite of their failings, these nuns who lived and fought and died over a century ago were heroines of God. They carried with them a faith that was capable of moving mountains. Oh, apparently they did not accomplish much according to the standards of our progress-ridden world. Surely there were times when the comforting convent walls of St. Walburga in Germany beckoned to them, when the hunger and cold that surrounded them forced their minds into a realm of discouragement. Yet, they trusted in God even when He didn't seem to be listening.

They never saw the results of their suffering and labor. Years of autumn leaves have settled snugly over their graves, and the figure of Christ on a cross looks down upon their final resting place in a quiet cemetery. They never saw the Benedictine convents that sprang up all over the United States as a result of the lives they so generously gave to Christ.

In our present day the temptations are different in

convents like the one in which these nuns lived and died. There is no longer want, nor heaps of snow upon our beds. Our anxieties and sufferings are of a nature peculiar to the time in which we live. Perhaps we are inclined to feel that we could serve Christ better in the world outside. Maybe the good we could do would be much greater than here where we begin to find a cloud of doubt dragging down our spirit. The modern trend is to be free of anything that might impede our newfound social awareness.

It is easy to lose our nerve, to shirk promises made to God when the whole world was bright. We did not dream that as time rolled on these promises would entail a life of strange uncertainty and insecurity. And yet they were freely given, and it is only right that we should keep them.

What if those Sisters a century ago had yielded to the feeling that must often have walked with wooden shoes across their hearts, begging them to slip away from this wilderness, pleading with them to go back to a country and people who understood them? Yet they didn't falter. They stayed and struggled with a life that to outsiders did not seem worth living.

Although we live in a difficult world, we still must realize that we never solve problems by turning from them to a land that repudiates personal responsibility and presents a face of cosmetic happiness and joy. We must stay at our post in rain and storm, remembering that heaven's King gave us an example when He hung upon the cross. He was a failure according to all standards. He had not built great cities, nor won battles. Christ had never gone to Rome or Greece, but stayed His whole lifetime in the backward country of Palestine. Yet He saved the world because He did His Father's will.

6

Faith Is a Gift

The senior boy in the CCD class was the type girls dream about — intelligent, with a football player's build, and a spontaneous gaiety that often flashed across his face like the sun's rays through a light misty rain. But on the day I am going to tell you about he wasn't smiling. His question was blunt, unadorned, "How do you know you've been baptized? You don't feel any different."

Since the beginning of classes in September I had felt as if I weren't reaching anyone, as if I were trying to call various people on the phone and the lines had all gone dead. I walked to the window and looked for a few seconds at the swirling autumn leaves. A wild desire reached out with sticky fingers urging me to run away from the question by using sarcasm or some other subtle adult warfare.

Something whispered that we don't explain religion with weapons like these. They just don't warm the heart. Maybe this teen-ager was sincere; I had to give him the benefit of the doubt. Looking at him I could not be sure of anything. Perhaps I imagined that I saw doubt, puzzled anger, indifference. Since I am no mind reader, I couldn't be certain. Or was it just a routine question thrown at a difficult adult?

It is hard to explain faith to someone, and although the boy's face relaxed, I felt somehow I had fumbled, that it really wasn't too clear. The answer that his baptism was on the church record would explain the first question, but I felt he already knew that it was. The reply, "Faith in Christ who said, 'He who believes, and is baptized, shall be saved,' " somehow didn't create a feeling of faith either. It was just a routine answer. Faith is a gift given to us by the King of heaven Himself. But how do you make this real to a high-schooler?

Doubts raced through my mind as we drove home through hills of golden-red reaching up and touching a pale blue sky. Maybe someone else could reach this class, could bring these girls and boys to see Christ and the wonder of His love. A friend had once told me that, although I would never admit it, I worked best when I had a challenge.

But was this a challenge, or was it perhaps a form of arrogance and conceit? I was trying to say, "Open sesame," but like Cassin in the *Arabian Nights* I had forgotten the password which would open hearts to the treasures of heaven. Apparently souls that I dealt with were not becoming keenly aware of Christ. He did not live in their lives. It was impossible to reach them, to show them the wonders of the vision faith gives us on the darkest night of our life. During the week I pondered faith as I read *The Silent Spires Speak,* by Father Raymond, O.C.S.O. It crept into the psalms I prayed during Matins. I brooded over it when I went to a second Mass with the eighth-grade boys, who give me the impression, even when I cannot see their faces, that their minds have stepped cautiously out of the door, and are mingling with the traffic of their everyday lives. Faith? What did it really mean to me? There was a day when I felt I could do much more spiritually in a different work, and had expressed the desire to the class I teach. The boys sat quietly as if stunned — a situation which does not occur too often. Then a voice from the back of the room said with shocking clarity, "We need you, too, Sister!" It was a cry that went straight to my heart.

And now, today, I wanted once again to feel the cool breezes of success blowing in my face, instead of the dry desert winds of failure scorching my mind. I was tired of fighting, and the smell of a spiritual battle lingered with me. The understanding and comforting Christ had been buried under a heap of bright autumn leaves as far as my mind was concerned, and I could no longer see clearly.

In all of us, I think, there is a weakness. Mine is a fear of spiritual darkness when everything has been grasped and held by the ruthless hand of failure; I wish to stop fighting. Mentally I retreat into my hermitage of spiritual peace, but is this where the God of love wants me — some place where there is no darkness, and I do not need faith?

St. Thomas, coming upon the Apostles that far-away day in spring, felt perhaps keen doubts. He had gambled that Christ was no ordinary man. He had thrown in his lot with this stranger. And he had lost. Hadn't he heard the wild cries of the men who hated Christ piercing the air? This man he had followed had hung there until He was dead. Perhaps that was the moment when faith died in Thomas' heart.

Now the Apostles wanted him to believe this wild tale of seeing Christ. How credulous did they think him? He had been around. He knew Christ was dead; no one ever survived a crucifixion. Did Thomas look contemptuously at the others, wondering how they could be so superstitious? He was a realist. And even though the Gospels do not say, I wonder how much faith he really had from the beginning.

When Christ stood before him in all His glory, the world changed for Thomas. There is no need for faith when we can see and hear and feel. And it was easy to murmur the words: "My Lord and my God." But the answer Christ gave in strong masculine tones that day has whispered a song of love down the ages for those who do not see or understand and still have faith: "Because you have seen Me, Thomas, you have believed; blessed are those who have not seen and have believed."

It isn't easy to go on from day to day with faith in a Christ we never see. In an age of communication and visual aids, our minds want to reach out and understand everything. We wish to touch infinity. We forget that the Christ who died on the cross when the darkness sowed seeds of doubt in the hearts of many, has risen. If we had faith, our spirits would forever dance to the comforting rhythm of the beautiful lyric, "In My Father's house there are many mansions, and I go to prepare a place for you."

7

Friendship Is a Risk

"Are you going to your room after supper? I have something I think you'll like." I turned and looked into the dark eyes of a younger Sister.

"Yes," I replied somewhat wearily. "Somehow, I'm just tired all the time." I was trying to get over the surgery I had undergone a little over a month before and the eighth-grade boys I taught weren't helping me to recover. It seemed that I had been sick and depressed for a long, long time, and there just wasn't anything I could do about it.

I hadn't been in my room long when there was a knock on my door. When I opened it Sister stood in the doorway holding a silver box. She held it intriguingly, as if it contained treasures. I forgot all about being tired, sick, about the boys I taught. The hint of a secret, and the eternal curiosity of Eve is enough to arouse any woman. I had to see what was in that box.

"Sit down," I said, eagerly pulling out a chair. Sister seated herself carefully, as if she were about to perform a major operation.

"Now," she said as she opened the box and took out a plaque wrapped in tissue paper, "this you can have, and

I don't care what you do with it." It was the serenity prayer. She must have known that I liked the prayer. Then she took out a small replica of an angel, saying, "I thought you'd like this, too." She dug deep in the box and rustled the tissue paper. I leaned forward wanting to see this last treasure, wondering.

Finally she got it out of its wrappings and handed it to me as if it were her most prized possession. It was a lovely statue of the Madonna done in pastel shades. I took it from her and examined it carefully, exclaiming over the exquisite hands, the gentle face. I knew this was something she valued, something she wanted to give me, and yet something she wanted to keep. She whispered softly, "I would not give this to anyone but you. I want you to have it. It was a graduation present. But if you ever want to give it away, give it back to me."

I looked at her closely before asking, "And if I break it?"

She smiled. "That I won't mind, but I just don't want you to give it away."

She left the room after chatting for a few moments. I found myself still holding the statue, awed because she wouldn't have given it to anyone else. Why had she given it to me? I was sure there were many Sisters in the community kinder and more deserving than I. Yet. . . .

"And if I break it?" I had asked. The thoughts ran helter-skelter through my mind. How easily something so fragile could be shattered accidentally or by someone's careless handling! I thought of when I used to climb the stone wall that separated our land from the Labarges when I was a child. Wild morning glories used to climb all over the wall. They were lovely dipped in morning dew, while the sun shone on their pink dresses.

But I had hardly picked them when their delicate

pink turned brown and they were dead. I always felt sad because they wilted so quickly. I have had friendships which turned out the same way. They were full of promise, and for the most part came quite suddenly into my life, but they never lasted. They blossomed overnight, then faded before the sun sank in the west.

Other friendships resembled summer. They endured heat and storms — the scorching sun of trial and error, and the winds of loneliness and uncertainty. They seemed to have become a part of me, but suddenly something happened and they were gone. Tears never could bring them back. Had I failed, or had the one I loved failed?

You and I are so funny in this regard. We fail in our friendships and refuse to admit that we perhaps were to blame. We say, "I will never trust anyone again; it hurts too much and I can't take it." It is as if I had said to Sister: "Take the statue back. It is a risk I do not care to take. It might be broken. I might forget and leave it in the sun, and its pale pastel colors may be gone forever."

Some friendships gather dust. Because we see these friends infrequently, if again, we forget to write to them, to call them, to let them know in any way that we love them. Maybe someday we will look at something which reminds us of them as I look at the statue of the Blessed Mother which reminds me of the Sister who gave it to me. It will make us wish we had let them know how much they meant to us. Meanwhile we chase the duties of life up and down the lanes of the world trying to capture something, we know not what, while these forgotten friends whisper brokenly, "Where are you? I need you."

Some friends endure the spring rains and the summer storms. They reach deep into our hearts and their touch keeps us warm. It is for these we would risk all. Like wine, their love has grown mellow as time passes. They are there when the frosts of autumn nibble at our peace of mind. They are there when the winds blow cold with a chill we find unbearable. They are always there stretching out their hands when trouble invades our lives. What would we do without the encouragement of these friends? They are a tremendous gift God bestows upon us.

One thing that makes us fearful about friends is the fact that we may lose them. Just as I said to Sister, "What if I break it?" so I say to myself when a new friend comes into my life, "What if this friendship should be broken? Am I ready to take the risk?" But regardless of the cost, isn't it better — in the words of the old saying — to have loved, even if we have lost, than never to have loved at all?

Friendship may grow, or it may fade away. That is a chance we all must take. If we are afraid of making friends because we may be hurt, we are not worthy of the name of friend. Even though we may form a friendship that is as fragile as it is beautiful and find some day that it is crushed and we want to cry, it is still worthwhile. We will be better people for it. But you and I want to play it safe. Will our friendship cost us inconvenience? Will it help us? Is it worth it? Will we be hurt? If we are worried about these mercenary trifles we have not learned to love people. We are simply using them.

There are hands that are reaching out to us every day of our lives, hands that ask for a kindly touch in a world that can be so bitterly cold and empty when no one seems to care. These extended hands are like the plea of our changeless Friend, "Behold, I have loved you always." Do we shake our heads sadly and walk away because we know that "I must give of myself before I can take anything"?

8

An Old Typewriter

A few years ago I made arrangements to exchange my ancient typewriter for a portable. Since I was not stationed at the motherhouse, someone else transacted the business, receiving the paltry sum of five dollars for my antiquated machine. I came home to find this piece of equipment in a neglected corner of the room. The salesman had not yet picked it up; perhaps he never would. As I stood looking at its old-fashioned carriage and dusty keys, a feeling of sadness crept over me. The tab didn't work; the bell had ceased ringing a long, long time ago; even the keys required a heavy touch. Yet I could put my head on this old machine when I was ill or tired. Often I ran nervous fingers over its keys when I was trying to think, and the thoughts seemed to have lost their way in the tangled streets of my mind.

Whenever I left the convent to teach elsewhere, eyebrows went up — was I taking my typewriter? Sisters on the same floor as I hinted that its loud clanking noise wouldn't be missed. Those going with me remarked significantly: "You aren't taking your typewriter along, are you? We have typewriters there, you know."

And now, when my eyes fell upon it on my return to

the motherhouse, I knew that its usefulness was at an end. I had pounded out the last play, the last article, the last letter. It was almost like saying good-bye to a faithful friend who was lost forever to me.

There are times in our lives when we look back to a past which is seated in a sunlit room of our minds. It has taken the coziest rocker, and as it sways back and forth it sings happy songs of the days that are dead and gone. The skies were bluer in those times, the grass greener. And God? Well, He seemed to be nearer to the people who strode through our lives. But was He? It was no easier to love God then. How our minds cherish and fondle those memories! We do not wish to mar any of them with the specters of failure, loneliness, or starless nights. We may even create a dreamworld if we aren't careful — one peopled with perfect beings who belong more to a utopia than earth. Are we to blame for this? It is hard to say farewell to a fantasy which wears golden earrings.

We forget that life is a journey to eternity. The thought that there is always the great love of the God who planned this trip through the deserts of the world should sink deeply into our very being. His strong arms are always there to hold us when everything we do seems to be filled with frustrations and broken dreams. The world in which we live changes with a swiftness which unnerves us. We become restless and reach for something to ease the stress and strain which buffet our minds.

It is then that we are so drowsy with dreams of the past that we stop looking for the God of the present. We stir up in our minds worlds moldy with memories and glance fearfully into a future of uncertainty. Is it because we lack trust in the Lord who so loved the world that He sent His son to save it?

We must remember when these disturbing memories

of the past insist on running through our minds that the magic of all the wonder God has given us is at our fingertips. There are birds singing in the summer, the sun leaving its rainbow colors in an early evening sky, frogs piping a silver cadence. Nature is at peace; we should be too, knowing that each day that passes brings us nearer to our meeting with the God who surpasses all our dreams.

Temptations, sorrows and loneliness must creep into every life. If these pass us by we would never remember the God of love, nor would we desire to serve Him. If suffering were absent for long, we would become spiritual cripples.

The years, months and days of our life offer numerous challenges. As we grow in age and wisdom, we also must grow spiritually. Since we are other Christs, we must expect to suffer the pain of misunderstanding, the wounds of apparent failure, the sharp sting of others' doubts. How could it be otherwise?

Perhaps we have forgotten the first Good Friday when a broken, bruised God-Man stumbled through the rough, narrow streets of Jerusalem accompanied by a wild angry mob, whose screams cut through the gentle wind like a sharp knife through pine wood. Even though this God's body was wracked with pain, He went stumbling on His way. He slipped, lost His footing and fell, but He never stopped. Why? Because He loved us. This is a truth filled with mystery. Why should He love us? We are so unlovable. Yet the magic of His love is always there, hiding in the shadows which grow solid in the earliest light of dawn. The future holds out to us a meeting with this loving God when the sun of our life here on earth has gone down in a night sky, and we meet the One who has given us His love in eternity. There is no reason to become tangled in memories when there is so much in the future.

9

If We Were All Alike

Sister and I were interrupted in the midst of our conversation by the banging of the screen door, and two Sisters running as if the house were on fire. One of them looked up and saw us.

"Brown's pig is loose. Come and help us chase him down to the farm."

Then she hurried on. We looked at each other in dismay. "You go," Sister said; "you know I won't be any help since I can't run."

I didn't think running had anything to do with a pig. They were slow, clumsy animals — dirty, too. But I went anyway.

By the time I reached the scene the pig was walking complacently toward the highway. Sister Lucile was making futile attempts to change its mind about going in that direction. She didn't seem to be at ease with the pig. "Shooo!" she would say, going forward one step and shaking her scapular, then retreating two steps. The pig ignored her.

I stood for a moment, not quite sure how pigs reacted either, then started to laugh softly. Although Sister hadn't heard me, she turned and said in a clear, disturbed voice:

"This pig is worth a great deal of money and if he gets on the highway. . . ."

Sister Mary, who was standing beside me, not knowing what to do either whispered wonderingly, "Look at the pork chops on that pig. I hope it doesn't chase us."

At this I came to life. "I don't know much about pigs," I told her, "but this I know: they won't chase anyone."

"Yes, they do!" she insisted.

"Oh, they do not. They — "

The argument was abruptly ended as the pig changed its mind about the highway and turned, then made a wild dash directly toward us. We didn't lose any time getting away. By this time a boy from the farm had come. The pig changed its course again and ran for him. He ran, too, just as we had done. We turned and watched to see what the pig would do next. It suddenly stopped and seemed to become calm; its ears flopping dejectedly, it followed the boy back to the farm. Since the show was over, the three of us went back to the house and entertained the rest of the Sisters with a detailed account of our adventures with the runaway pig.

Today with the wind sighing itself to sleep outside my window, and the snowflakes falling from the sky, covering everything with a layer of quiet beauty, I think of that day filled with laughter. There is so much I can draw from that humorous incident. Perhaps what we thought when we were there, watching the pig, not knowing what to do, is the most important.

As Sister Mary mentioned, one of us thought of the practical angle, the other of food, and I had seen only the humor in the whole affair. Now suppose Sister Lucile had decided that we should all think as she did. If she had said, "You should be more serious; in this world where people are starving, you shouldn't take the death of a pig so lightly," I would have been more amused.

Or suppose one of us had been interested in zoology, and had felt that everyone should make a study of this animal. All this sounds quite absurd perhaps, but I wonder if we don't want everyone to think and act as we do where God and religion are concerned.

Isn't that what some of us do in religion? It becomes a drudgery where the love of God ceases to be a joy. We dwell on cold little experimentations that we are convinced will save the world. Some of us have our particular plan and we want those around us to think, act and dress just as we do. Sometimes we seem to forget that the ideas, dreams and ideals of each person are different, that this is what makes life exciting and novel and filled with adventure. There are many roads which lead to God, and if someone wants to take a route which he finds is better for him than the "new" theological highway, isn't that his own spiritual business?

We can never be quite sure of the future. That is why we must go to God in the way we know best, the one that fits our emotions and makeup. Oh, we may be very wrong in our views and outlook, but that is a chance we have to take. We aren't like anyone else in the whole world, so why try to conform to a carbon copy? Just as in this absurd little incident I told you about, I think difference in people makes life interesting. To me it is the hand of God making each person colorful with His grace. The Holy Spirit guides each one in diverse ways.

Those persons with whom we come in contact each day are fascinating, unless we decide we are going to do an upholstering job on their ideas, so that we can put them in an unused parlor of our mind, feeling we have done them a great favor by pressurizing them into our way of thinking. If we have done this, if we have managed to force someone to depend only on what we think — nothing is gained.

We have stood in front of a mountain and refused to let a mountain climber go up simply because we personally fear mountains. There are different ways of doing this. We may convince him that he is taking a chance, that he'll never make it, or we may use our greater strength to keep him from it. So he never climbs mountains; he just stays in the valley with people who are even afraid of climbing hills for fear of falling.

When Christ came to earth, those who believed in Him did not all use the same method to get to heaven. The Good Thief did it in a very dramatic way. He asked Christ to remember him when He entered into His kingdom, and stole heaven. Mary Magdalene went to Him and braved the stares and sneers of Simeon's guests, which may have appeared foolhardy to those who knew her. Then there was Peter who became the head of the Church. He wasn't always correct in his thinking, but I'm sure he never tried to be just like John who seems to have been a born diplomat. They were all friends of Christ, but they didn't all try to think the same. Each one was unique.

And it seems to me that if we try to make those we come in contact with become like us in thinking and acting, and succeed in doing so, we will find that our world has become a world of puppets, who respond to our pulling the strings. Then the variety of thoughts and words and actions will have vanished, and we will live with strange unnatural people with personalities of drab browns and greys for the bright coloring in their lives will have disappeared.

10

When You Need Someone

My brothers have always been near to me, even though sometimes years elapse between our visits. They have always understood me best, seeing my weaknesses and shortcomings clearly. Many memories of them are stored carefully in the soft gift-wrap of my love.

The oldest and perhaps most practical of my brothers is Rod. Once when my mother was very sick, and my world rocked with worry, he and I had a long talk. At the time, he was far different from the brother who used to show up in the uniform of a state trooper when I was a child. Then he awed me. In my childish way I looked upon him as a sort of Prince Charming.

But now when we conversed together it was quite different. The uniform was gone; so was his youthful gaiety. In its place was a wisdom and understanding that led me to talk freely with him. There was no reserve or hesitation as I poured out all my anxieties into his willing ears. Now and then he would make a comment. When I finished telling him all my worries, I felt relieved.

Oh, I was quite sure there wasn't too much he could do. But he had sympathized, had given me his full attention. I wanted to put my arms about him, to tell him how much his love meant to me. But I refrained because I knew that this would have been an embarrassing display of emotions to my brother. So I just said, "Talking to you has made me feel much better, Rod," and smiled.

There are days when life takes on a dark blue mist, when all sunshine seems to have fled, and we feel terribly alone. No one can really help us or guide us right. Even in the midst of crowds laughter is hollow and we feel alone. We want to run away to a different time, to another place.

But the God of Calvary who dwells in the tabernacle will listen to us. We can pour our hearts out to Him, and unlike our fellow humans, who, with the best intentions, cannot help, He will and does. We may not feel any different; in fact we may wonder in the darkest room of our hearts if Christ has even heard our cry.

It is then that we must have a tremendous trust, reasoning within ourselves that God is there with a strength and a power that know no bounds.

In our age of quick communication we no longer want to wait. We hurry from one thing to another like the rabbit in *Alice in Wonderland,* always looking at our watches, forever asking ourselves if we have used every moment of our busy day. It is so easy to become creatures of time, missing the voice of the timeless Christ.

The space age has done much to destroy our patience. We forget the words of the blind poet Milton: "They also serve who only stand and wait." So, in our impatience to accomplish great deeds, we miss the little things that are all about us. We trample on the Mayflowers of kindness in our hurry, and the opportunity to pick them never comes again. There are many unimportant people in the world waiting for Christ in our smile, our word, our gesture. We hurry up and down the highways of life like robots, concentrating our attentions on what are supposed to be the great opportunities while the insignificant events of everyday living go unnoticed. How selfish we can become without being aware of it!

In our great rush we have even lost our sense of humor. Yes, I think many people are so absorbed in being up-to-date that they have forgotten how to laugh. Life is a serious business, but does it have to be gruesome, unadorned with the humaneness of love and understanding?

Our hearts become heavy and without hope. The grim business of merely living takes on steel armor and a helmet which shuts out the music of laughter, the sound of singing birds, and the pleading of human voices.

Perhaps if we could remember that Christ is all strength, while we are all weakness, it would make us see ourselves as we really are. We are not someone who will set the pulse of the world throbbing wildly because of our importance. But each one of us can be great in the little things. The spark of hope we have lit in the heart of some person by our smile or just a simple word of kindness perhaps will be the greatest gift we can present to God.

Like Cinderella when the clock struck twelve, we force our hearts to go into a practical world of hopelessness. We are afraid of dreaming dreams since they might never come true. We are afraid of loving anyone more than just a little because we might get hurt. There are so many things we are afraid of, including the fear of loving the Son of God too much. Even our prayers become fluttering words that set up echoes in the chambers of our hearts. We do not wish to risk our reputations by becoming conspicuous friends of God. But, if we are not God's friends, we cannot really be anyone's friend.

11

He Seemed So Far Away

My brother Joe had made me angry that day. When I started to cook dinner I had asked him to go to the store for something special. He teasingly refused. I was giving him a whole list of reasons as to why he should go. But, there were no answers coming from the living room, so I went to the door and looked in to see if Joe were still there.

He was there all right, but he was sound asleep on the couch. Now I was irked since what I was saying was nothing like a bedtime story. After mashing the potatoes I put the dinner on the table and called Ed who was reading the paper on the front porch.

We sat down. Ed looked at me and said in a puzzled voice, "Where is Joe?"

"Asleep," I replied impatiently.

"Well, aren't you going to wake him?"

"No! He can sleep all day for all I care."

Ed looked at me closely but said nothing. We started to eat our dinner. I took one bite, then another. After all Joe hadn't done anything really bad. The whole thing was rather silly. Everything would taste awful when it was cold.

I put down my fork, got up from the table and went

into the living room. "Joe," I said, shaking him, "it's time for dinner."

He got up and followed me sleepy-eyed to the table. Ed looked up, but said nothing. Amusement crept into his eyes, and a broad grin spread across his face. He didn't have to say a word for his expression said clearly, "I knew you couldn't let him eat a cold dinner."

The years passed and the scenes shifted. Joe became an officer in the navy; Ed died shortly after I entered the convent. As the years passed Joe would show up at the convent for an occasional visit. However, a convent, perhaps, is not an ideal setting for renewal of family intimacy. The visits seemed cold and formal as though he were exploring the planet Mars while I sat on the edge of the moon dangling my feet. The distance between us seemed to grow and during the past year I took the magic carpet woven with happy memories of Joe and tossed it into a crater of the moon.

There was no use dreaming over a dream that had lost its warmth, a dream that was years away in another age, another place — better to forget it. We were leading different lives in different worlds.

One evening, a short time ago, the phone rang. "Long distance," the Sister who answered it said. It was Joe. His voice was the same as it had always been — mellow, soft and filled with laughter. Immediately I was under the spell of brotherly affection I knew of old. We chatted easily and pleasantly. Suddenly his voice changed, and he said, "Tell me honestly, are you really happy?"

I stiffened, and something in me went cold. His words showed clearly that he was well aware of the turmoil taking place in today's religious world. Joe had never thought the wisest move I ever made was entering the convent. In fact, the first time he saw me as a nun he told me frankly if he had been home he would have tried to talk me out of it. And now. . . .

Intensity crept into his voice, a quiet strength that had always pulled me up when I was discouraged: "You do just what you think is right! You do what you want to do."

Then somehow the passing years were forgotten. This was still the brother who had been close to me before I entered the convent. When the conversation came to an end, my heart was singing. If Ed were looking down from the eternal hills he would have chuckled, and said: "He never lost his power over you, did he?"

On a much larger scale all of this is much the same as my relationship with God. Sometimes when I kneel before Him, it seems that He is so far away, so unreal. I say to Him: "You gave me a religious vocation, God. For You I gave up those brothers who were always there to shelter me from the rain. And my friends? I was just happy to be around them. Now You don't even seem to be listening. You seem so far away."

But He really isn't far from any of us. He comes in the most unexpected ways. He comes in the silence of the night, in the song of a bird, and sometimes in the deep loneliness of our human hearts.

Even now can't you hear Him whisper: "I have loved you with an everlasting love"? Isn't that enough to keep a song of love always in our hearts?

12

I Loved Sister Marigold

The Sister of my story was not really Marigold. However, since a younger member of the community has inherited her name I will give her this one, because to me she was really "Sister Marigold."

It was the middle of the afternoon when I looked from the window at the rock garden which I wasn't really seeing. From the infirmary I could hear the low murmur of nuns' voices in prayer. Sister Marigold was dying, and I was alone in the community room. Although I did not see or hear her I was suddenly aware that someone was standing beside me. When she spoke, Sister's voice was puzzled: "Aren't you going to join the others in prayers for the dying?"

I shook my head. Sister went on: "But you were so close to her. I thought — " It was then I turned and looked at the Sister beside me. "Please, Sister, I don't want to see her," I said, with little sharp edges running all over each word.

A surprised look stirred in Sister's eyes, but she only said softly, "All right," and slipped away. Once again I was alone with my memories — memories that I wanted to keep free of the breath of death.

Sister Marigold had been an invalid for more than twenty years. I had carried her trays and, since she was practically blind, written and read letters for her. One day I had come home from school to find an older Sister waiting for me. Sister Marigold wanted to see me immediately. When I entered the infirmary room she turned her head and asked, "Is that you, Sister Jean Marie?" And then without any warning she began to cry. I went over to the bed and she took my hand. "Sister said you would come, even if it isn't your week for trays. She said I could depend on you. I wonder if you would write a letter for me."

Once when I carried her tray and greeted her with the usual, "How are you, Sister?" the cheer that was so much a part of her seemed sunk in a dark blue cloud.

"Oh, Sister, I wish God would come for me. I'm no good to anyone here."

I tried to comfort her by saying, "But, Sister, you are. Who would pray for me if you didn't?" Putting out her hand she whispered: "I would. I'll never forget what you did for me, and I'll get you into heaven too."

There was so little I had really done that I felt ashamed, and yet she was so deeply grateful that she would promise to reach down from heaven and help me to get there.

Now, I'm sure the Sister who found me standing alone the afternoon when Sister Marigold died didn't understand my reasons for not joining in prayer with the rest of the community. Yet, she didn't insist, didn't ask questions, didn't try to enforce her opinion upon me. Perhaps she even felt a touch of rudeness in the way I answered. But she was too much of a lady to intrude. She knew that this was my decision — that I had a perfect right to it.

In our world today people blatantly pride themselves on their understanding. Yet, if someone does not go along with their ideas he is considered gauche, he just "isn't with it." Refusal to allow for individual differences is certainly not the equivalent of understanding. Do we really understand anyone? How can I say, "I understand," when I am so complex that I do not even understand myself? If we believe that we have a secret formula for getting to heaven, that does not give us a right to force it on someone else.

A short time ago all this manicured spirituality depressed me; now it amuses me. When someone says, "I really don't understand you," I grin and say, "You really don't have to, you know."

None of us will reach heaven in the same way. A person who is suffering from arthritis does not take the same medicine as someone who has a heart condition. The same is true in the spiritual realm.

Although I do not care for folk Masses I do not frown down upon them. It is simply that I prefer the Mass where I feel free to express myself in prayer without any outside influences. Guitars make me think of dancing; they entertain me, but they do not refresh me spiritually. But, really, isn't that a personal opinion, something I have a right to feel?

When spiritual shadows stretch their arms across our lives, we may, or may not, want to share our difficulties with someone. In our day, when we are trying so very hard to be do-gooders to all men, I wonder if perhaps we frequently stretch forth hands that are merely cold and dry. Perhaps our neighbor wants to work out his problems for himself.

The dreams that people dream are their own, even if they do not correspond with our dreams and ideals. If they wish to remain in what they think is an exquisite valley of hazy blue where they find God, why try to make them climb mountains that may only place a film of frost on their hearts and minds? We are so busy watching to see whether a person is going to share our views that we miss seeing him at all.

Saki's Francesca says: "I pride myself on being able to see other people's points of view." Her author explains that she saw her own point of view from various angles, while they all confirmed her settled opinion.

The sharp old face of human criticism will always be with us. It is often unaware that it is trying to project its opinions and ideals and ideas into our minds. We must learn to laugh at all this, to continue loving the world, and never take ourselves too seriously.

In the winter we may look from our windows and see the moonlight on fresh snow while the sound of the wind is soothing to our ears. A few nights later the magic may be gone for we only see the snow whirling angrily and hear only the mournful sounds of a cold wind. It is much the same with our spirituality. Sometimes we feel that we can almost reach out and touch God. Prayer is easy and heaven is just a hop, skip and jump away. Then again we may feel a spiritual fatigue which pulls us down, and there doesn't seem to be a God at all.

What I am trying to say in all this is that we must accept others and ourselves as we are. When Christ hung on the cross that first Good Friday He accepted everyone just as they were. His Mother, Dismas, Magdalene, John, and all the others were extremely different. It would have been a real tragedy if Christ had said to Dismas, "Now, you look at John. He's always been a good boy; he never robbed and murdered and. . . ." Christ never made comparisons; He just loved — including a thief to whom he said, "This day you will be with Me in paradise."

IV

Winter

*Silently, like thoughts that
come and go,
The snowflakes fall, each one
a gem.*

— W. Hamilton Gibson

1

Winter Winds

As we drove through the hills that had been transformed from gray winter into a shiny white fairyland, I thought of the first Benedictine Sister I had ever met. She stood quietly in a sheltered corner of my memory — working at a hooked rug, watching me intently with brown eyes, while every now and then she inquired about my first two years of high school.

From the very first moment we met, something sprang up between us — it was the birth of a friendship between a dignified, calm nun and a skinny, uncertain high-school girl.

The day I graduated from high school she told me I would someday come back and enter the convent. Nothing was further from my mind. The world was covered with stardust that day, while the magic of its spring breezes blew from my mind any desire to live the hidden life of a nun. But I did not want to awaken Sister from her dream, so I only smiled.

It was more than two years before I saw Sister again, the day I entered the convent. Our meetings were few after that, yet I always had a feeling she was watching me from afar, expecting the best I was capable of giving, feeling for me when things went wrong as they sometimes did. Deep within me there was a hope that I would turn out to be a little bit as she would like me to be.

A few years ago my friend was removed from the list of assignments. Often we exchange a few words, and sometimes we have a long conversation. She mends my clothes with the same love and attention with which she taught me geometry in my high-school days. Sister has now reached the quiet snows and cold whistling winds of late life. It is a waiting for Someone who has loved her in time, and will do so in eternity. Gone are the songs of birds and the soft spring winds which sang melodies to her heart. The warmth of summer meadows under sunny skies are past. Autumn leaves singing their songs of farewell on still fall days have vanished. But, in spite of all this, I believe that Sister hears the voice of God riding in the wind on winter nights.

Older people find that their step is not so brisk as it was when they were younger, nor are they as alert. Physically they slow down, but in their hearts there is a stirring of comforting love. They know that someday in the near future the snow will melt, the sun will shine and they will meet the God of love who will introduce them to a land of eternal spring.

Just as the seed of spring wheat is buried from our sight, so is the humility and joy of those who have loved God for a lifetime. In the twilight of their lives, when God is near, how much wiser they are than when the whole world stretched out eager hands! They once looked at life with the joy of a small boy examining his treasures in a chest. In those days their minds were always on the verge of uncovering a world-shaking mystery.

Now the spell has vanished, but in the hearts of those who have grown old trying always to love the Son of God there is still magic. Bodies grow feeble and trembling, but hearts that are united to Christ grow young as eternity approaches. They have listened and heard the echo of the night soft and gentle with a warmish wind.

We may feel lost as the twilight days of life approach. This could be brought on by not trusting or loving God when the moments of trial leave us groping in the dark. When the journey toward heaven is nearing its end, we should, I think, have a deep longing for God. It may be cold outside, but in our hearts we will allow His wishes to be accepted. The world may be indifferent to us but our hearts will be warm with the acceptance of His wishes. Our last winter days should be like a fairy story with a spell of wonder coming ever closer — an enchantment which must be broken only by the voice of the Son of God.

Around us there will always be cold, logical people trying to force us to focus our attention on a stiff, practical world. But our dream of the coming of the King will keep our hearts warm and contented on the coldest days of winter.

Christ once said to Peter that when he grew old He would take him by the hand and lead him. Did this not show a spiritual childhood of old age that would be a lantern to light the way for those born in other generations?

It seems to me that Christ was reassuring Peter that when shadows and piercing chill crept upon him in the form of years, He would still be there to help him. There would be no moment of panic, even when the snows of winter piled over the windowsills of his heart. In the unbelievable silence all around, Peter could listen for a voice that would transfer him into the realm of a new life.

In our quest for knowledge, which we often mistake for wisdom, let us remember that God is not dead, that He dwells eternally in the hearts of all who permit Him even in the coldest days of winter. As Emerson once wrote in a poem pertaining to winter — a poem that reminds me of Sister:

> Over the winter glaciers I
>   see the summer glow,
> And through the wide-piled
>   snowdrift the warm rosebuds below.

2

Somebody Needs You

It was one of those stolen moments during Christmas vacation. Ideas were floating about my mind begging to be written down, asking me to take care of them before they disappeared into the land of "No-Returning." My fingers were just beginning to move over the keys of my typewriter when there was a knock.

Now a knock at the door at ten o'clock in the morning can bring any kind of intruder. It may be someone who wants me to walk to town, some work that has to be done immediately, or almost anything. I have thought of putting a sign on my door reading: "Please go away, and don't bother me now. My mind is occupied with thoughts that are slipping by fast."

But knowing the Sisters I live with, I am sure this would cause amusement. There would be many knocks asking me why I put up the sign, and comments about its practicality.

"Come in," I said in answer to the timid tap.

In walked a Sister whom I didn't know very well, someone who had never sought me out before. I was puzzled. At first the conversation was very casual, but it became clear after a few moments that this wasn't why she had really come. Her remarks were an introduction to something she wanted to tell me, something that was really troubling her. But I had to let her come to this in her own way, without rushing her.

Once, without thinking of what the look would imply, I glanced at my typewriter, and I saw all my ideas drifting slowly into the air. She didn't seem to notice. Finally she began to talk about the real reason for her morning visit. The clock on my desk ticked away quietly, while the morning shrank into a different pattern than I had planned. When Sister left, it was time for the Rosary which I usually pray just before dinner. All my inspirations for writing had grown cold and disappeared into space. However, in spite of all this, my heart was glad. Before leaving, Sister stood at the door and said, "You've helped me so much. I needed what you said today." And then she was gone.

Somehow I think the Annunciation came to Mary in a very ordinary way, without warning. She had perhaps planned on doing something else with her life. Isn't it true that in our hurried days we may not hear the sound of God's voice speaking to us through our neighbor?

As Mary looked and listened to the clear, concise message of the angel, did the cry of Isaias rap sharply on her heart with its forebodings of what would face her if she accepted this invitation?

"I that speak justice, and am a defender to save. He was clothed in a robe sprinkled with blood, and His name is called the Word of God."

The angel stood in all his heavenly splendor waiting for the answer of the girl from Nazareth. But there was only one answer, to do the will of God regardless of the changing of plans, and in spite of the suffering it entailed.

At that moment when earth was embraced by God,

did Mary catch a glimpse of some of the heartbreaking trials that would be hers in the future? Did she see the green hills of Nazareth change to a barren hill where the body of her Son hung on a cross, nailed there by the people He had come to save? Or was she unaware of the type of suffering that would be hers?

The words of the angel were brief, and he departed, leaving Mary alone with the most unique secret the world ever had known or would know. Yet everything about her seemed the same to her neighbors in this rustic town. They had known her gentleness and love, but her real apostolate remained a secret.

In our restless time we seem to feel that we must reach out and touch a world. Yet, I think, perhaps we forget those about us. They knock at our doors with demands on our time, and we show them by our words and actions that they are interrupting our busy lives, and we wish they would leave us alone to carry on our "good works" with those we have never seen. In so doing, we miss the opportunities of the present.

When Sister said, "You've helped . . .," I felt small and ashamed for the feeling I had when she first came to me. How unimportant the writing I was doing appeared when compared with helping someone, and yet I almost let the opportunity lose itself in lesser things.

The rumblings from Jerusalem and other important places were heard in Nazareth. Fear drained the courage from some hearts, leaving a vast emptiness inside of them. Mary went on living among them, listening to their woes, loving them. She heard the sound of the weak, felt their sickness and loneliness, their despair and hope. At the end of the day, did she perhaps pull the cloak of love around her a little tighter and ask the One who dwelt within her to help by making the world less cold and empty for those who had sought her help? We have to try to give of ourselves regardless of how we feel. We cannot turn from people even when the muscles of our souls have become taut, while it would be much cheaper and safer to ignore them. Like Mary, we must grow in love for the world around us.

3

Silent Loveliness

The windows in chapel this morning did not keep back the tiny snowbanks piled along their ledges. Our prayers and the Mass were accompanied by the wind which whistled hungrily against the stained glass, demanding to be noticed. As we came out of chapel the small sign "All Schools Closed!" attracted everyone's attention and caused miles and miles of smiles.

It brought back memories of when I was a child and my father used to come into the kitchen where we were waiting to hear his verdict as to whether we would stay at home or go to school. He was always very dramatic about these announcements — taking off his coat, blowing his nose which was red with the cold. Then he would put sadness into his voice as he said: "You can't go to school today; the snow is too high." I loved those stormy days, and I think I will always love them even if I grow extremely old and am confined to a rocker.

During the morning I looked out of the window only to see the snow piled in gleaming miniature mountains along the street. I had promised a Sister at the hospital I would go to see her soon. The practical part of me told me to forget it, but I had given my word. After dinner I walked out into the great silent loveliness. The storm had raged most of the night and morning and was still playing havoc through the streets. Most of the sidewalks had been shoveled. Before I had gone far I saw before me a stretch of virgin snow that seemed forgotten. Should I go out into the street to avoid it or . . . ? A man moved before me without any warning. With ease he plowed his way through the drift. When I was a little girl I had always followed my brother's footsteps on the way to school. Without another thought I tried walking in the man's tracks. His steps were too long. Snow slid into my arctics and slipped gleefully around my ankles in a cold, wet ooze.

At the end of the drift of snow I came face-to-face with the man whose footsteps I had been following. His smile and greeting seemed to imply that he wondered what I was doing out in the storm. I helped the cause by saying, "Only someone as foolish as I would venture out in this storm," then pulled my shawl more tightly around me.

A quizzical look flickered over the man's eyes as he gave the indifferent reply, "Well, if you have to go out, you have to go out."

That was all the conversation we had as we both moved back into our own private worlds. But since the magic of a winter's day was upon me, it did not matter what the stranger thought. I trudged on with my own thoughts of happiness.

We do not see the dreams and ambitions, the sorrow and gladness of people with whom we come in casual contact. They are often buried like the landscape on a stormy winter day beneath the still beauty of snow.

I like to think when Christ was apprehended in the garden, that there was laughter in His heart when men, over whom He had complete power, tied His hands with a rope. One cannot tie up Infinity in shackles. It is free. The will to live and love and find a response to His love was deep within the human Christ, yet no one saw it. He loved with the wildness and strength of a fierce winter storm. None of us can understand a love that would let itself be taken by an angry, heartless mob, when that love could have chosen a much easier way to save mankind. And yet, somehow I like to think there was music in the heart of Christ, even when He was suffering all the cruel, unnatural torture that the men of that time could devise. This was His winter with a people He had loved so well. How were these poor misguided people to know as they led Him from the garden that He was their God? How could they know they would stand out in history as the ones who inflicted punishment on a God who had come to save them? These people were not alone. We were there, the unloving part of us — the part that refuses to forgive and forget. The selfishness which hides under the cold of self-respect, and refuses to let the power of God's unfailing love melt its icy edges, has tied His hands through the ages.

How strange that we should always blame the crucifixion upon those who took Him in the garden when we are so far removed from love! Time can warp our love if we aren't careful, and make us stiff and cold like snow in the middle of winter. We become painfully aware of the mistakes of others, but never blame ourselves.

But this King who let Himself be tied with the ropes of man's lost love has left us with a challenge. We must always see Him in those we meet each day in spite of storms. Even when our hearts seem to be freezing and the music is faint, we must remember God is waiting for us in individuals who are suffering the cold of hatred and the icy grip of unfairness. He waits for us as we walk up and down the avenues of life.

Are we perhaps too preoccupied to notice the tears of the stranger, the outstretched hand of the beggar who waits in vain for a few kind words and a smile to heal his heartache? Are those around us dying from lack of love?

God is waiting for us to take Him out into the stormy hills of life, to find Him where the winds of passion blow. Are we willing to brave the wind and cold for Him?

4

Our Songs Are Gone

January has a way of chilling my spirits. Christmas has come and gone. The shepherds have trekked back to their windswept hills; the kings to the mysterious East. The last bell has jingled its merry tune before being packed away among bulbs, holly and other Christmas ornaments. Soft fleecy snowflakes have been replaced by severe storms and icy winds.

Perhaps all this "let-down" was the reason for my deciding to put on a play. The principal stared at me when I suggested it. "It's a sailor play," I informed her. "Patriotic — you can use it for either Lincoln's or Washington's birthday." Sister appeared unconvinced, as if she were not quite certain of what was going on in the dark corners of my mind.

But it really wasn't patriotism that made me want to do something different. It was the slump everyone seems to get into at this time. The play would fill the vacuum January exams created after the heartwarming songs of Christmas ended.

Occasionally spirituality is a little like a January day. We hear the sound of music in our hearts; then it is gone and we find ourselves grasping for a memory that has vanished, or refused to let us catch and hold it once more in our hearts. The God of Bethlehem has become a refugee in the deserts of Egypt — deserts which seem to be close to every moment of our existence. Warmth and tenderness have been blown away by a cold wind whistling through barren trees.

We feel during days like these as if our spirituality has become as weak as thin cardboard. We must search for Christ, since we do not find Him in a cave on a lovely night which is filled with the light of the stars and a pale crescent moon. It is necessary to use the shield of faith to keep materialism, secularism, and all the other "isms" which seem to be descending upon mankind out of a "Pandora's Box," from invading and upsetting our spirituality. We must keep them from wresting from our will all the warmth and love in our possession.

All through the lonely January days, when the love of God is more a sigh than a word, we must struggle against bitterness, when our spiritual life appears to be filled with futility and pain. Even if our wings have been clipped, and we are grounded in a land of ice and snow, a land which we neither know nor understand, since our whole being seems to be frostbitten, we must never let the song of Christ's love leave our hearts.

This is His world, and these are His people, puzzling though they may be. Christ, the Light of the world, still loves us. In moments of trial, when faith in Him has been trampled upon by a pleasure-seeking society, we must refuse to sacrifice our ideals at the bargain counters of the world.

We must search through the ominous clouds of darkness for the love of God which breathes through us. The half-whisper of "God is dead" should never even stand on the doorstep of our hearts, in spite of the bitter, hysterical voices bidding us in no uncertain terms to forget about Him.

In the dark hours of the morning when I cannot sleep, I think of Christ that far-away night in the garden with the chill of loneliness heavy upon Him. To whom could He turn? Even the three Apostles He had loved so much were asleep. Because He was God He knew that Judas was about to hand Him over to his enemies, using the sign of a kiss to make Him known. How the human in Christ must have struggled to withdraw during these excruciating moments of mental torture! How He must have longed for a ray of light!

But there was no light, only the deep darkness, and the sound of the wind in the trees. His heart was filled with pain, while the name "Judas" slipped brokenly from His lips. Life had battered and warped Judas, and had spun an untidy web around his heart — a web which was only interested in material things. How Christ winced with pain at the thought of what lay before Him! He must have wanted peace more than He wanted anything at that moment.

The Son of God saw Judas against the dark sky, hair ruffled, his face in the hideous grimace of one trying to act the part of a friend. Yet, Christ did not run from the garden into the tranquil silence of the night. Instead of using what the world would call common sense, He refused to flee, but remained to receive the kiss of a treacherous and obviously avaricious person.

We must remember this when the stress and strain of modern living places a heavy hand upon us. The days we live in are strenuous and difficult. At times we sense that we are living in a postcard album with quickly turning pages which lack warmth and tenderness. But it is a world that we can never run away from, even when we feel terrified at what the future will bring. Like Christ we must go on, even when everything seems hopeless and our courage is waning.

5

Life's Problems

I had just written my name on the commercial arithmetic test paper when I heard Mr. Tadd's voice: "The formula for the first problem must be stated."

For a moment I sat and tried to remember, but I couldn't, so I decided to work the problem before writing the formula. I was almost finished with it when I heard an angry voice say: "I told you to write that formula!"

At this point I could feel the tension all around me; it seemed, too, that I could almost hear it. Mr. Tadd and I had never been on friendly terms, and perhaps that is why I answered sharply, "You never taught us this formula!"

If I had tried, I couldn't have said anything worse. The air was charged with electricity. "Miss Langevin, I don't care if you pass this course or not. You can fail the test if you want to."

Since I didn't answer, he left and went back to his desk. My mind cleared; I worked the problems, and then went back and figured out the formula. That was the end of the communication between Mr. Tadd and me for the time being.

A few minutes later, while fumbling with my locker, I heard a masculine voice behind me: "If you come over here, I'll show you how to work that problem and the formula, too."

I turned and said coldly, "You don't have to. I know how to work it."

Tom's eyes widened incredulously: "Then why didn't you do it?"

"Because when he yelled at me, I forgot everything I knew. Anyway, I'm dropping commercial arithmetic. I won't pass it, and there's no use my wasting time going to the class."

"But if you drop it, you won't get a diploma. You're in the secretarial course, aren't you?"

"If I didn't pass, I wouldn't get it anyway," I argued unreasonably.

"Well, why don't you find out what your marks are before you drop it?"

"Oh, all right, I'll find out, but it's hopeless," I answered impatiently, because I really wanted Tom to get lost and stop giving me advice.

A day later I told Mrs. Sullivan the whole story. It had improved and grown gradually worse. By now I was sure I could never pass.

"But you have to have commercial arithmetic for the course you are taking," she explained. "Let me check your grades."

In a few minutres she returned, looking puzzled. "I don't know what you are complaining about. You got 100 in the last test, and your other marks are high."

"Thank you," I mumbled, too startled to say more. The whole world looked bright again. I went off to thank Tom, determined that I would never let anything like this upset me again.

This was a futile promise to myself, for I never have learned to take things calmly and to think over them carefully and deliberately before I act. It has been this way in teaching, in writing, in everything I do. Something goes wrong, and I am ready to quit, to push everything aside and begin something new. But practically every time this occurs there is someone who steps into my life as Tom did — someone who almost forces me to look at the situation calmly, to think it over before I do something foolish.

God has helped me through those with whom I live and come in contact each day. I know I am really dependent on others. If no one took the time to make me look at what appears below the surface in these disturbing moments, I would do foolish things and be sorry afterward. When I am standing in a Bluebeard's chamber and my emotions are aroused — anger, discouragement, a feeling of futility — I am very apt to flounder around in confusion with a lost perspective. At this time, when my mind is in disorder, God sends someone who opens the door. This person thinks logically and restores my sense of balance.

We tend, do we not, to be self-sufficient, to feel that we can do things independently of others? We will solve our own problems quickly and efficiently, run our own world in the best possible way, without having to depend on others. Their opinions are as unwanted as a moth flitting over the folds of a red velvet curtain hanging in back of an altar. Oh, people are well-meaning but we just can't be bothered. They wouldn't have any idea what is involved in our life. We build our own silent worlds, feeling that shadows of doubt will never fall upon their walls.

There are times in life when there are no stars in any of our nights, nor are there any dawns, only a drab darkness where we stumble about in search of the right answers. It all seems about as useless as looking for the pot of gold at the end of a rainbow. It is at times like these that God sends someone. It may be a personal contact, a passage in a book we read, a movie, or any other kind of communication. Our mind clears, and we can think our problem through. Often this keeps us from doing something we would be sorry for in days to come. Nor should this make us feel weak. It is like the sun lighting up the dark corners of a house which has had its drapes pulled for a long time, bringing out the good in those with whom we travel on our journey toward Eternity. God shows Himself in the kindness and help He gives us through them. He sends His messengers of love to bind our wounds and soften the blows that are given to us.

We can become our own worst enemies by refusing to recognize that we all are inextricably dependent on others. It will always be true that "no man is an island unto himself." Life may bruise us through people, yet we must not dwell too long on these words that cause pain, otherwise we will forget the many who have come to our rescue with the soothing balm of thoughtfulness.

6

Hope Lights up Dark Places

Since it was my fourth year of teaching at the CCD center, I felt I knew the position of every piece of furniture, every window, and certainly every door. Someone was waiting for books which were in the supply room. It was dark, but I didn't bother with lights. Like the courtier in the story "The Lady, or the Tiger?" I was very sure this was the door. I opened it, reached for the light, then fell. I felt my arm strike the hard concrete and then a stabbing pain. I neither screamed nor reached out to stop the fall — I just couldn't understand how those steps happened to be there.

When I finally landed at the bottom of the thirteen steps, I tried to figure out where I was. Then I thought of the two Sisters with me and the pastor. Would they find me unconscious, with broken bones? Darkness was all about me. It came to me that this was a part of the center I had never explored, never even entered. I got to my feet, reached down and picked up my veil. The air was heavy with dampness, and the musty smell was anything but pleasant.

Reaching for the stairs, my hand touched emptiness. My sense of direction was gone. I stood motionless, knowing that I must have light or I might stumble and hurt myself more. So I called four times — each time my voice was a little higher, a little more desperate. There finally was a light, and an anxious voice asking if I were hurt. I climbed the stairs; there was no need to explain. My disheveled appearance spoke volumes.

There are times in our lives when we seem to have fallen spiritually into a dark cellar. How we arrived there does not matter. We stand alone and bruised in spirit. Hope has grown cold, and we cannot rekindle it. We reach out our hand and touch the cold cement of materialism. Our sense of direction is gone. Fear lays clammy hands on our shoulders, while we know not where to turn.

Could it be that in this darkness the greatest hazards are empty words like commitment, involvement, renewal, relevance, dialogue? Surely now, if ever, is the time to ask the Light of the world to renew the lamp of hope in our hearts.

Apparently we will never again feel young spiritually, nor have the soft breeze of spring melodies blowing gently over our soul. Hope lingers for a day on the doorstep of our hearts, then it is gone. Something whispers that we should give up, should cease trying. But is this what the King requires of us — a loss of hope in Him because we no longer see Him in the gloom?

The book of Job tells us that "life is a warfare." But it says much more. It teaches us to hope when the windows of heaven seem to have blackout curtains.

It is easy to keep in step when paths lie safe and sure. But sometimes we enter a danger zone where doubts, fears and temptations raise their heads, while tentacles of anguish reach out for us like a giant octopus to grasp and hold us in their power. A trapped apprehensive feeling spreads to every corner of our hearts.

Somehow I feel that the greatest darkness on Calvary

was not in the blotting out of the sun, but in the fact that most of those whom Christ had loved and touched with His kindness had disappeared when He needed them most. "Oh, yes," some of them may have said, "He was good to us, but after all, haven't the high priests condemned Him?" It was an easy way to soothe their consciences. Hope was gone and the lights in the windows of their hearts had been blown out when they saw what kind of a King He was.

So they went back to their humdrum lives; they opened the wrong door and fell into a pit of darkness. But somehow, I think nothing could ever blot out from their minds the memory of that memorable Friday when the lights went out on Calvary. Christ had touched their lives and they would never be the same. They could not love Him as they should. Yet no matter how hard they tried they could never forget the Figure on that cross.

7

To Be Or Not To Be

It was a time when spring was waiting to replace winter — a time when spring is about to sigh before coming alive with fresh green grass and blue skies.

Connie's party would have been most enjoyable for me, if it hadn't been for the decision I had to make. That is why I slipped away from everyone and went down to the edge of the lake where I looked over its dark waters. On the other side, somewhere in the darkness, was Birlington, but I couldn't see it anymore than I could see the future. The unrest in me was growing, and I could no longer dismiss it. What should I do? Was there anyone in the world who would understand how I felt? Jim always understood me. He was here; all I had to do was return to the party. Why hadn't I thought of him before?

As soon as I got back to the party I heard his voice. "Come over here. Where have you been? I want to talk to you."

What he said I don't even remember. It was like a record I had heard again and again. In the middle of his conversation I blurted out, "Jim, I've been thinking of entering the convent. What do you think about it?"

His mouth dropped open a little, and he stared at me

in disbelief. If I had said I was going to enter an institution for the retarded, he wouldn't have been more astonished. He put down his glass, then looked at me as if he were seeing me for the first time.

"You what?" he exclaimed, as if words had been playing pranks with his ears.

"Enter the convent," I said dully.

"Why, you'd never fit in a convent. Whatever put that in your head? Are you trying to be funny?"

By this time I knew I had made a mistake. Jim, with his Methodist background, would never understand this. He was under the impression that anyone entering the convent was disappointed in love, running away from life, or slightly deranged. Telling him this hadn't been such a bright idea. This was one decision I had to make alone anyway. Not only Jim, but none of my friends would understand anything like this.

"Now you listen to me. How could you adjust to that kind of life? You like parties and people and you're so alive. You're just not the type; *you're not the type....*"

Jim went on and on, never stopping for breath, and I was too weary with the whole idea to argue. When he finally asked, "Shall we dance?" I was relieved.

The magic had gone out of the night. It seemed that I wasn't sure of anything anymore. The price I had to pay in giving up the world rose to gigantic proportions, and I wanted to cry. I knew, too, that I had overestimated Jim's understanding. I had been abrupt in introducing him to a world he knew nothing about. Since he liked me, he wanted to prevent me from doing something foolish, putting a blight on my life, twisting it until it was no longer recognizable. And the strange part of it was — I felt Jim might be right.

There is a spiritual winter which descends upon us

just before the green twigs of spring stir in our hearts. We are uncertain; we have been struggling for a long time; the disturbing whisper of our conscience has forced us into unknown worlds of ice and snow. We are tired of the people around us. Those we should be able to depend on do not seem to understand us, and we are thrust straight into the arms of sudden decisions which can be made only by ourselves.

I knew after I talked to Jim that I could not take his advice and be true to myself. At the present time I know that I cannot live at peace with myself by following the advice of those who feel that they are prophets and have all the answers. Jim was in good faith when he advised me not to enter the convent; he was as sure as anyone could be that this was not for me. After all, I had really asked him what he thought. It hadn't occurred to me that he didn't know the first thing about nuns; therefore, he wouldn't be able to help me. It was like asking a lawyer for medical advice.

Sometimes we overestimate the help those around us can give. We go to them, state our problem, then find that instead of solving it for us they intensify it. Surely it solves nothing to be angry with them. They are looking at the whole thing from a different point of view. There are some problems we just must figure out for ourselves.

There are well-meaning people who believe we are incapable of helping ourselves and offer their advice when it isn't wanted. Occasionally they become very angry when we do not respond as if they were oracles sent straight from God to put us on the right path. This is unfortunate and may cause pain. Yet we have no choice. It is the price we must pay to be at peace with ourselves.

The thief on the left of Christ drew up terms of surrender for Him when he taunted: "If Thou art the Christ, save Thyself and us." This to the thief was the sensible thing to do. But Christ didn't follow the plan, practical as it may have seemed to the thief and those witnessing the crucifixion. This was what He had to do to save the world: He had to die so that it could live.

Where principles are concerned, there is only one true solution: do what we think is right, regardless of what those around us may think or say.

8

Out in the Cold

Peter and I sat in the guest house and talked. He was a nephew of mine and had come to town on business, and was staying in the guest house for the night. Minutes passed without my knowing. When I am carrying on a conversation I forget all about "time." Finally I consulted my watch. It was after ten and I had work to do before I retired. Reluctantly I said good-night.

When I went outside everything was dark and strangely quiet. I tried the door of the convent and found it locked. There was no use trying the window; I knew the Sister who had charge was always careful to lock it. I turned and started for the main entrance to the convent. Peter loomed up before me in the darkness, his voice concerned as he asked: "Are you locked out? Do you want me to go with you?"

"No, Peter," I replied with hope in my voice that didn't betray my anxiety; "I'll get in somehow."

Although it was almost spring, the night air was filled with a winter chill as I walked quickly around the building to the front door. I rang the bell again and again, but no one came. Through the door window, the long hall looked still and deserted. The full moon came out from behind a cloud, while stars glittered in a velvet sky, and I shivered as the cold crept through me. The whole situation seemed hopeless, so I turned and retraced my steps, trying to figure out a way to get into a convent that seemed to have every door and window closed and locked for the night.

"If you are ever locked out, call to me and I will come down and let you in." I suddenly remembered one of the Sisters saying this to someone else a month ago; at that time I wasn't even vaguely interested. But now perhaps a Romeo and Juliet act could be performed at a staid Benedictine convent.

The moon was still shining as I stood below her window. It was lighting up everything, dressing the rock garden with its silvery beams. But at the moment I wasn't too artistically inclined; I saw no magic. All I thought of was getting inside where I would be out of the cold. This was my only hope. If Sister didn't hear me, I'd have to sleep in the guest house.

"Sister Enid," I called as quietly as possible, but with desperation in my voice. Again and again I called her name. At first everything was just as it had been. This window as well as all the others looked at me with hollow eyes. Then there was a movement, and a moment later Sister Enid was at the window.

"Sister Enid," I said with relief tripping all over my words, "I'm locked out."

"I'll come down and let you in," were the most comforting words I had heard in a long time.

A few minutes later I was inside wrapped in the arms of warmth and solace after the chill and discomfort of the night. How terrible it was to be out in the cold!

St. Luke's words, "He arose and took the Child and His mother, by night, and retired into Egypt," came suddenly to my mind. When she went into Egypt, Mary was, in a way, locked out also. These were her people; this was her land; yet, she was being exiled to a country she had never seen, one she did not understand. It was not a matter of minutes, or a few weeks or months, but years before she could return to her country and to her neighbors. How her heart must have ached for the familiar sights of Nazareth, for its friendly greetings! This country, where she had been sent by God, was one of floods and spawning mud. Hates, cruelties and hideous gigantic gods hid in this land of helpless people. Mary saw fear in sunken eyes and she was keenly aware of the poor who did not know where to turn. The sun beat down mercilessly upon piles of sand which smelled of hot stale air. At night the cold winds chilled bodies to the bone.

It was quite different from the soft breezes of Nazareth where the air was sweet. And she was lonely for the friendly ways of her homeland — its songs, its laughter; yes, even its heartbreak. But God's will for her was even in the stifling wind that came from desert sands. She knew peace, even in her sense of loss. When hostile, suspicious eyes looked up at her with dark distrust, she recognized the need behind those eyes and tried to comfort and cheer these people with ideals and dreams so different from her own.

Years slipped past while she waited for God to send them back to Nazareth. Yet she knew her Son had come upon the earth to save those who worshiped the true God.

God is still with us when we are locked in a world of darkness where the gods of pleasure, wealth and power seem to hold full sway. We live and breathe the air of conflict all about us. It seems to us at times that hope has ceased to burn, leaving nothing but a blackened wick which twists and smokes within our hearts. It is then we must call to the Mother of God for help, just as I called to Sister Enid on the night when the whole house seemed closed against me. She will whisper to our tired minds brief words of assurance — words which will keep the light of hope from dying in a world of encompassing darkness.

9

Love Is That Way

It was one of those mornings when the sidewalk was a sheet of ice. I stood at the door and looked across the short distance between the convent and the church. My fear of slipping on ice had developed by leaps and bounds through the years since I had spent a week in the hospital with a broken ankle. "But then," I thought, "this ice shouldn't keep me from going to Mass." So I went creeping over it like an old Mother Hubbard.

All went well until I reached the church door, and then I fell. There was a sharp pain in my wrist. I must have uttered some sort of exclamation for one of the Sisters was at the door asking if I were hurt. Now there was nothing else to do but straighten my veil and go into church.

Father came out and started to say Mass. Wild pains chased each other up and down my arm, my head felt light and my stomach was in an unhappy condition. All the typing and work I had to do came rushing to my mind. "It isn't broken," I said to myself; "it can't be."

But I remembered all too well what I had taught in various first-aid classes, nor could I shut out the echo: "The signs of a fracture are swelling, pain, deformity.... You may have only one or two of these but...." I moved my fingers; it increased the game of tag. The signs were there. The pain had been there from the first and now I detected a slight swelling.

I wasn't praying — just feeling sorry for myself. How could I do the library work with one hand? How could I type? Why had I been so foolish as to try walking on that ice? There was no answer. I couldn't turn the clock back an hour and not venture out of the house. I never have been one of those noble souls who prays for crosses, who begs God to suffer for Him. It isn't even the easiest thing for me to accept the trials He sends.

A preview of what a broken arm would entail passed through my mind that day. I knew what was before me: pain, inconvenience to others (I have an independence deep inside of me that dislikes asking anyone for favors), X rays, a cast, trips to have the doctor check. All of this made me rebel a little. And yet, the wrist was broken. There wasn't too much I could do about it.

Many of us, I think, tend to be overanxious about the past. We worry so! We make mistakes; we say things which we regret, but can never recall; we fail; we have our own particular temptations and fight our own spiritual battles. Most of us dream of building towers which reach to the sky, and they fall before they are even well-started. We think if we could begin a new life with new circumstances, things would be different. But would they?

God has put us into these times, these circumstances, given us these people to help us work out our salvation. But you and I wish to change the scenery. We want our own props, our own carefully chosen characters. We are so funny; so changeable. Today we pray like a second-century martyr, tomorrow like a fiery crusader. Although we do not notice it ourselves, we change. Was life really meant to be placid for any of us? Was it meant to be as sunny and calm as the lake where I used to swim on clear days before I was a nun?

We are living in a fast-moving world, one that places demands on us that play havoc with our nerves. Sometimes it bewilders us. Yet, should it make us unmindful of those around us?

As someone wrote to me a short time ago, something I hope he does not mind if I share with you: "Response, it seems, is one of humanity's besetting defects — we fail to listen; we fail to answer because we are absorbed in our egocentric thoughts. . . ."

Why become so absorbed in our work that we cannot see the signs of a lonely heart, a tired body, pushed almost to the breaking point? Our failures and faults are always with us, they always will be. We cannot turn back the pages of time, even if we wanted to do so. But we can start each new day with a resolution to love more, to give more, and that is really all that God asks.

While all of these thoughts tumbled about in my mind I thought of Christ in the garden when Judas advanced with arrogance begotten of stupid duplicity. Judas, with a mob at his heels and betrayal in his heart. Christ did not run away from the cross that lay before Him. There was only an offer of forgiving love when He asked softly: "Judas, do you betray the Son of Man with a kiss?" No resentment here, only the kindliness of a God, One who is all-merciful.

Christ was not concerned at that moment with Himself, only with those around Him. He would go on to Calvary, but His Apostles must escape. How intensely human when He told Peter to put up his sword! He did not chide Peter for being foolhardy enough to think he had a chance with the temple guard, or explain to him that the odds were against him. He knew that Peter's bravado was an act of love. And love, no matter what the price, is beyond even God's chiding.

A short time ago a young priest who was a wonderful speaker told me: "You may not know this when I am preaching, Sister, but I get violently ill. I have thought of asking my superiors to remove me from this work, but that would be running away. It is a price I must pay for my spiritual success." Love does have a high price tag. As Father Raymond, O.C.S.O., has written in his book *These Women Walked with God*: "You do not live until you love. You do not love until you give your heart away. You do not give your heart away until you have found *God*. Then you live and love because you walk with Him who is Life and Love, and you know the happiness for which you were made. . . ."

10

Memories of Mr. Arno

It was one of those cold, still January days that takes your breath away and leaves you with a creepy contradiction: external exhilaration and internal depression. I was watching Mr. Arno load milk cans in the back of his old jalopy. I used to ride to school with him, and on the way I told him all my troubles. To me they were gigantic. Mr. Arno never shrugged his shoulders, or made me think they weren't. He was always concerned and appeared deeply interested in what I said.

When I didn't go to school for several days he always made me feel I was missed by asking: "Were you sick?" (I think I was sick during my eighth grade more than all my other school days put together.) But this particular morning I couldn't wait until we got in the car to pour my woes into his sympathetic ears.

"Paul's awfully mad at me," I said.

The clatter of milk cans drowned out my voice.

"What did you say? I can't hear you!" Mr. Arno yelled.

So I yelled back: "Paul's awfully mad at me. I took my mother's fountain pen when I went to take my regents yesterday and lost it."

He put a can down and looked at me closely. "Why should Paul be mad? What did your mother say?" Then he went right on banging the cans while I kept right on yelling.

"He gave it to her for Christmas. Neither my mother nor my father is home."

"Oh, so that's why Paul's so high and mighty."

I should have been consoled, but I wasn't. Paul was considerate, and I didn't blame him for being angry. First of all I shouldn't have taken the pen. Besides it was careless of me to lose it. I was just full of misery. It was cold standing there, but I wanted to talk to Mr. Arno, not that I felt he could do anything about it, but he was such a good listener. I pulled my collar up, thrust my hands into my pockets and sighed. All I said was, "No, it's all my fault."

When we got into the car Mr. Arno said, "Now don't you worry; we'll find that pen. I'll drive slow and we'll both look for it."

Although I didn't tell Mr. Arno I cried, and that the tears froze unhappily on my cheeks, I think he knew. Even though he was driving at about fifteen miles an hour the milk cans behind us chattered like teeth that resent the cold. We had gone only a short distance when he said, "There is something black on the right. Do you see it? Get out and see if it is your pen."

The world around me was suddenly filled with magic. It was the pen! My heart was light again. When I got into the car Mr. Arno was smiling. "See," he said gently, "I told you we'd find it."

Mr. Arno needed a shave and he certainly didn't smell of cologne, but to me, at that moment, he was a knight in shining armor.

Years later, when I was a nun, my mother wrote: "Mr. Arno died last night." I felt a pang of loneliness as I opened the door of an almost forgotten memory. God, I was sure, would be generous with this big rough man who had time to listen.

It is strange that in our modern world so many of us have forgotten to listen. In our sophisticated society we lack the human touch. If we do take time to hear what people are saying, we are inclined to make it clear that we are not too interested. Yet the people we meet each day are waiting for our smile. They hunger for an encouraging word, but they go from us empty-handed. These are the riches none of us are too poor to bestow. No one is so poverty-stricken that he cannot take time out to be considerate of those whose hearts beg for understanding. Peter once said, "Gold and silver I have not, but what I have I give to you. . . ."

Perhaps you will say Mr. Arno was uneducated, from a different age, but I disagree. He was educated in the language of the human heart. He did not have to drive slowly that winter morning, nor offer me any sympathy, but he did. Kindness fits in every age, nor do I think our education is complete unless it has opened up the door of our hearts. But you and I are so busy getting insignificant things done, that we overlook the importance of those with whom we come in contact each day.

Our own problems take on gigantic proportions. We forget the gracious word and generous smile for which some heart is hungry. We hurt people by neglecting them, then justify ourselves with the empty words: "I didn't mean it that way." We search for great deeds, scorning the tiny acts that light candles in our neighbor's eyes.

Mr. Arno was unlettered, but he was a spiritual giant. If he had read this he surely would have thought my making him a hero was a joke. Yet he taught me a valuable lesson the day after I lost my mother's fountain pen; a lesson which I never could have found in books. He taught me a unique lesson in love. It is a lesson which warms my heart even after these many years, and I am no longer an impressionable little girl.

Sometimes I think that Mr. Arno was closer to "getting with it" in Christ's way than we are today with all of our blatant "social commitment."

11

The Nun's Story

I was preparing to leave the community room to catch up on some long-delayed correspondence when one of the Sisters said, "Stay with me and watch 'The Nun's Story.'"

My reply was: "Sister, I've seen the movie, read the book and written an article on it. I'm not particularly interested in seeing it again."

A nun's voice from the doorway joined in, "It's from the dark ages," then she closed the door softly.

I laughed and sat down, saying, "I'll stay for a while, but not for the whole thing."

We had missed the first part of the story, but it was easy to gather the fragments that we hadn't seen. I had not watched the movie long, before I was looking at it by the light of the lantern of Vatican II.

The story revolved around a Sister Luke. The nuns in her convent were Stoics in every sense of the word. Where Hollywood ever found all the wooden-faced women to put into the movie I'll never know. As soon as the door closed upon Sister Luke for the first session of indoctrination, a sour-faced Sister in an emotionless voice made it clear that she should forget about being human.

There was no "love" mentioned, no crucified God-Man who would always be there to help — only a set of rules and regulations and meaningless practices. The superior who had apparently forgotten about being human said: "You can fool us, but you can never fool yourself and God." To make a candidate enthusiastic was definitely not a part of the superior's philosophy of life — if she had any.

Although this movie and story have been fictionized, many people believe every part of it as convent-truth. In doing this chapter I would like to pretend that the story actually happened just the way it is written.

Sister Luke soon discovered that her convent provided an ample supply of human icicles as a substitute for love and she slowly drifted farther and farther into that remote land where loneliness was the only wind which blew through her heart. She tried to travel a road that was rough and hard without the strength of the God who had loved her enough to die for her.

She became more detached from reality as the days wore on. She tried to find compensation for spiritual emptiness by putting her whole heart into nursing. In her artificial convent, strange rules (like not touching anyone) were more important than charity; so, when a fellow novice who was leaving the convent came to say good-bye, Sister Luke refused the extended hand and walked up the hall close to the wall, showing, according to inhuman instructions given her, that she was humble.

While I was watching this, memories of a personal experience flashed through my mind. When I had temporary vows I contracted a contagious infection and was in isolation. No one except the Sisters in charge of the infirmary were permitted near me. One morning as I lay tossing in fever I looked up and saw a companion novice standing in front of my bed. "Sister Ellen!" I exclaimed in alarm. "You're going to get killed if you're caught!"

"I don't care. I just had to see you. I wanted to know how you are. I brought you a glass of chocolate milk," she said miserably.

I was so sick that the chocolate milk was no more tempting than frozen soup when I was well. Even though Sister Ellen had been warned, she came; and it worried me. When she left I listened until her footsteps died away. I knew then that she was safe. Comforted by knowing that someone really cared, I fell into a dreamless sleep.

Some people might judge this incident as a conventual sin, but I would never agree. Sister came to me because she loved me. It was a human risk she had to take. And yet in Sister Luke's book of rules I would have been guilty of serious misconduct in not reporting this infraction.

This Belgian nun dreamed of lands where there would be no superhuman spiritual struggles. She hoped that in going to the Congo she would get away from the pettiness of her convent life and become absorbed in nursing. Desperately she wanted a spiritual paradise where her talents would be used. Deep inside of her was a growing need for appreciation, a hunger for the uplift that even a slight touch of affection gives to mortals.

In the Congo, where she thought to escape from herself, an attractive doctor brought her inescapably back to herself. He appreciated the rebellion that made her different from other nuns. It must have been wonderful to have someone on his staff who thought for herself instead of the other Sisters who were like well-oiled machines. They never gave him any trouble, but were dreadfully dull. Time and again she argued with him vociferously, but — his appreciative attention fell on soft, fertile ground. Sister Luke sensed her attraction to this man, but she would not admit it even to herself. It couldn't have been otherwise — she was starved for love, and her spiritual diet had been deficient.

Contrary to public opinion even a nun needs love. She can bury herself in work, she can become so devoted to religion that she is a living expression of it. Yet, she can never escape the demands of love. A Sister has no choice — she either falls in love with God and sets Him up in the throne room of her heart or she finds another idol.

Sister Luke had been trained in a convent of zombie-like spirituality where love lay dead and regulations and traditions were deified. Her spirit was never free to love God. Her heart was empty of hope, and somehow I keep wondering how different the story would have been if somewhere someone would have taught her that the true religious life is loving God even when the future blinks mockingly at us. It is trusting Him when the world about us seems to have woven an untidy web around our hearts. It is believing when our dreams have been destroyed and we no longer see the stars.

12

The End of the Road

It was a still, cold day when I visited Elk Haven — the home where people go when shadows are falling on their lives, and they begin to long for the joys of the eternal spring. I wish I could have taken you along with me and let you see the people there as I saw them that Sunday.

There was the lady who could not talk, who held out trembling hands to me and made inarticulate sounds that wrung my heart. Also there was the administrator — kind, gracious, understanding all these people who had stepped into the waiting station she had charge of when the backdrop of blue lights and soft music had disappeared for them. Just her presence lit candles in eyes that a moment before seemed devoid of life.

But the one who really impressed me was a frail little Italian lady. She talked rapidly and gesticulated expressively in the familiar manner of people who speak her native tongue. (I do not understand a word of Italian, so I merely nodded, smiled, and occasionally said, "Yes.") The woman beside her finally volunteered a few words: "She always talks Italian, then she gets mad at me. She says, 'Why do you never say anything but "Yes"?' "

The little Italian lady turned quickly. Her eyes

flashed threateningly and she spoke rapidly in Italian. They sounded like angry words, but neither her friend nor I understood. Her seeming anger was gone as quickly as it had come. She continued talking to me, almost begging me to listen. The other lady shrugged indifferently, and a tired, resigned look crept into her eyes.

The short time I spent among these old people will linger in my memory for a long, long time. For most of them it was winter at its end. The days must have dragged on and on as they felt life moving out of them. Did these men and women at the end of the day find fragile gladness in memories that had been a part of them in the spring and summer and autumn of their lives? Perhaps these memories were broken now, and they no longer wanted even to think of mending the pieces of those bygone days when life had been sweet.

Such tired winter days come to us spiritually and mentally even when we feel physically strong. We seem to speak a language no one understands. Memories do not stir our dull hearts to an appreciative response. We seem to walk under dull gray skies while the pure snow of winter that once stirred our hearts with its sparkling virgin beauty is gone. In its place are rivulets of cold water with dirty, slushy snow.

It is all so strange, so unreal, that if we are not careful we will become hard and dry, looking for a happiness that is wrapped in time instead of eternity. We cannot allow anything to sear and crack the soul's armor of love in a world that has grown cold in its material practicality.

We must be God-centered and full of faith, recognizing any diseased, warped materialism in our twentieth century. When spiritual winter descends upon us with all its storms and raging winds, God seems far away and scarcely real. We become intoxicated with selfishness, hardly recognizing the fact that whatever we have and are was given to us. We must love Him to be at peace with ourselves and the whole world.

When Christ hung scourged and spiked upon a beam, there was no one to understand. The crowds below Him had forgotten to keep a tryst with Him. How could they believe in a self-proclaimed God with battered knees and twisted feet, when even His own had deserted Him? A few of the soldiers were even quarreling about His robe.

Was this the man who said He was the Son of God, and cured their sick and blind? Winter in its worst form had come upon them. They could not understand the language of love Christ was speaking from the cross, and many of them — as the freezing cold of spiritual winter enveloped them — shrugged their shoulders and went their aimless way.

We must not leave Christ who offers us eternal spring when all our spiritual streams are covered with snow and our dreams are frozen stiff with ice. We must remain true to our King in spite of all this. If we listen to our hearts where we have allowed Him to hold full sway, we will find Him in a spiritual springtime where winds blow softly across the fresh green meadows, and ice and snow are gone forever.